Native Plant Landscaping for

UNIVERSITY PRESS OF FLORIDA

Florida A&M University, Tallahassee
Florida Atlantic University, Boca Raton
Florida Gulf Coast University, Ft. Myers
Florida International University, Miami
Florida State University, Tallahassee
New College of Florida, Sarasota
University of Central Florida, Orlando
University of Florida, Gainesville
University of North Florida, Jacksonville
University of South Florida, Tampa
University of West Florida, Pensacola

University Press of Florida

Gainesville · Tallahassee · Tampa · Boca Raton

Pensacola · Orlando · Miami · Jacksonville · Ft. Myers · Sarasota

Native Plant Landscaping for
Florida Wildlife

Craig N. Huegel

26 25 24 23 22   6 5 4 3

Library of Congress Cataloging-in-Publication Data
Huegel, Craig Norman.
Native plant landscaping for Florida wildlife / Craig N. Huegel.
p. cm.
Includes bibliographical references.
ISBN 978-0-8130-3494-2 (alk. paper)
1. Wildlife attracting—Florida. 2. Wildlife habitat improvement—
Florida. 3. Endemic plants—Florida. 4. Native plant gardens—Florida.
5. Landscape design—Florida. I. Title.
QL59.H86 2010
639.9'209759—dc22   2010015129

The University Press of Florida is the scholarly publishing agency
for the State University System of Florida, comprising Florida
A&M University, Florida Atlantic University, Florida Gulf Coast
University, Florida International University, Florida State University,
New College of Florida, University of Central Florida, University of
Florida, University of North Florida, University of South Florida, and
University of West Florida.

University Press of Florida
2046 NE Waldo Road
Suite 2100
Gainesville, FL 32609
http://upress.ufl.edu

This book is dedicated to my parents, Jack and Louise Huegel, who first set me on the track of wild things, armed only with their patient encouragement, not knowing where the path might lead but confident that I would find my way, and to my wife, Alexa Wilcox-Huegel, whose encouragement and faith provided the gentle prod to put these words to paper. In addition, in appreciation for their willingness to travel with me all over the state during their childhood and for tolerating my constant quizzing of plant and wildlife identifications, I want to dedicate this work to my three sons: Tyler John, Nathan William, and Evan James Huegel. Your company all these years has meant more than I can adequately express, and you have made me proud in a great many ways.

A male Northern parula warbler looks for insects attracted to the flowers of a tickseed (*Coreopsis leavenworthii*), Florida's state wildflower. Photo by Christina Evans, with permission.

Contents

4. Water in the Landscape 89

5. Plant Selection 95

6. Landscape Design 241

Preface

Natural Florida is an amazing magical place. Few areas in the nation are more diverse or mysterious. Although the seasons pass here with greater subtlety than in regions to our north, a beauty and complexity lie beneath the surface unmatched by any other. We are fortunate to live here and should embrace the natural wealth that Florida has to offer. Instead of shying away from it, we should insist that our developed landscapes capture more diversity and more mystery than is currently the case. What better place than Florida to recapture the sense of place lost from the areas where we live and work? Armed with a palette of native plants virtually unequalled in natural beauty and textures, we can be equipped with no better arsenal to fight off the blandness and artificial character that we have, for some reason, created and learned to accept. We need not accept the status quo. It has not worked well for us anyhow.

As urbanization becomes an increasingly familiar backdrop to our lives, many of us sense the need to reestablish connectivity to nature. We see problems with the traditional landscape approach that relies heavily on turf grasses and a limited number of overused, non-native trees and shrubs. We are bored by the sameness that greets us each day as we pass through our neighborhoods. We grow weary of the pretense that Florida is tropical, and we tire of spending huge amounts of energy and resources to keep it looking that way. We want to simplify, and we want to get more in touch with nature and with natural processes. We want our landscapes to do *something* besides simply serve as window dressings for our homes. We want more life in our landscapes, and we realize that we need to provide more meaningful habitat for wildlife if we are to get it.

One gains a sense of urgency and satisfaction by providing a place for wildlife around a home and place of business. The urgency arises on understanding the impact of Florida's rapid urbanization on our native fauna.

A 2003 study of the state's land-use patterns showed that nearly 4.1 million acres had already been converted from native land to some sort of urban development. This total is staggering, as more than 1.5 million of these acres were converted during the preceding decade. In more visual terms, the total acreage of urban landscape in Florida is now nearly equivalent to the land area of Miami-Dade, Palm Beach, Orange, and Hillsborough counties added together.

Aggravating these impacts even more, our patterns of development make it even more difficult for wildlife to survive because we have erected a monumental maze of roadways and infrastructure to link us together. Such infrastructure creates significant roadblocks in the movement and migration pathways required by wildlife. With land development, we have dramatically fragmented the historic expanse of unbroken habitat and relegated it to smaller, now disconnected blocks. Many species of wildlife cannot navigate between these isolated blocks.

If we look ahead to the additional predicted effects of global climate change on Florida, we clearly recognize that our current system of preserves and parks will be ineffective without the addition of real habitat to currently developed landscapes. Although Florida has the most effective and aggressive land acquisition program in the country, we must incorporate developed landscapes into the conservation equation to maintain the current diversity of native plants and wildlife; thus, creating landscapes where wildlife can survive is much more than a hobby. It is a significant modern-day conservation initiative.

The satisfaction in landscaping for wildlife comes from our inherent interest in wildlife and our desire to help. According to research by the U.S. Fish and Wildlife Service, Americans spend more than $4.3 billion each year on wildlife-related items (feed, feeders, etc.) and activities (e.g., wildlife-watching trips). These direct expenditures lead to additional spending—meals and lodging, for example—that pumps an estimated $29 billion annually into the national economy. As a nation, we are fascinated by wildlife, and we want to actively help. We want closer contact with birds and butterflies and other wildlife. Having wildlife around us is simply enjoyable. It enriches our lives. If we are successful at improving our landscapes to provide for wildlife, it will be fun.

A juvenile pileated woodpecker stops to investigate. Many species of wildlife will take up residence in yards if their habitat needs are met. Photo by Christina Evans, with permission.

Few experiences are more enriching than watching a pair of birds build a nest and complete the process of rearing their young. Some of my earliest wildlife memories are of peering through the living room window to monitor the progress of an American robin nest, waiting for the day when the young could fly. Many of us have, in turn, used this same experience to teach a reverence for nature to our own children. The realization that we have provided the habitat in our yards to produce this chain of life makes our landscape efforts even more satisfying. By adopting a new approach to the home landscape, we create opportunities for experiences that are priceless: the sight of a hummingbird hovering and darting down the buffet of flowers in a hummingbird garden; the magical transformation of caterpillar to butterfly; the high-pitched quavering trill of a screech owl as dusk settles in.

Although Floridians want to help wildlife, our efforts to date have not been especially effective. Nearly 45 percent of Florida's 668 resident vertebrate wildlife species continue to decline, and almost 150 are listed as endangered, threatened, or species of special concern, despite the fact that we spend nearly $63 million annually around our homes for such things as food, feeders, and birdhouses. The problem is that our spending has not been directed at what is important. We have not targeted the full habitat equation in our efforts, only small pieces of it; therefore, much of our money is simply wasted. If we are to truly help wildlife, we need to focus our efforts on providing habitat.

It is time we developed an effective approach to assisting wildlife in the areas we personally manage: the developed lands around our homes and workplaces. With more than 4 million acres to work with, we have our work cut out for us, but we should not be deterred from taking action.

Florida has the third-richest diversity of native wildlife of any state in the nation because it also has the third-richest diversity of native plants. Plants and wildlife are inseparable. Landscaping is the framework of the composition of wildlife occupying an area. Landscapes create habitat, and habitat is dependent on native plants. Effectively incorporating native plants into developed landscapes and reestablishing the essence of natural diversity can do much to eliminate the monotony and lifelessness of the typical urban setting. If we truly are interested in assisting Florida's

A female Northern parula warbler stops to cool down in a shallow backyard pond. Water features can be irresistible to migrating songbirds and other wildlife. Photo by Christina Evans, with permission.

wildlife, we are called and challenged to take a more eclectic approach to landscaping.

Now is the time to transform traditional landscape design to a higher art form and incorporate the elements needed by other living things to survive. Landscaping for wildlife should not be considered a hobby for the few, but a practice of the mainstream. It should not be relegated to "backyard wildlife" programs, but spread across all corners of our neighborhoods. It should not be considered a choice between maintained or unkempt, or between good citizenship vs. code violations and neighborhood shame. Wildlife landscapes are often no more than simple plant and design changes. They do not require eliminating aesthetic appeal.

In fact, the result is often far more interesting and intriguing than what we have become accustomed to, and getting there is both fun and richly rewarding.

It is my hope that this book will help you in this quest to change our approach and make a difference. This book is both a guide to assist you in selecting native plants for their wildlife habitat value and a starting point for understanding the components of landscape design that will make your plants more effective. No plant is entirely devoid of wildlife value, and no landscape will be devoid of wildlife, but some plants and landscape designs are clearly better than others. Your planting choices will have a profound influence on the types of animals that live near you, so you will want to make informed decisions to make your gardening efforts most effective. Use this book to help restore habitat for the native wildlife so frequently lost in the typical urban landscape.

Acknowledgments

This book has changed considerably since a previous one was published by the Florida Native Plant Society more than a decade ago. The author wishes to thank those who helped in its early form, especially Peggy Lantz for encouraging it and for providing editing and publication direction, the late Herbert W. Kale II, for providing a careful review of the initial manuscript, and my former colleagues at the University of Florida, Wildlife Ecology and Conservation Department, especially Joseph Schaefer and Frank Mazzotti, for providing an environment that allowed me to explore ideas. Since that time, numerous individuals have provided the input and assistance necessary for this revised and expanded text; most notably, Richard Wunderlin provided an early review of plant taxonomy, information about plant distribution, and, along with Gil Nelson, provided thorough reviews of the initial draft. The final product is much improved because of their assistance, and I am deeply grateful to them. Lucinda Treadwell provided an especially thorough edit of the manuscript and made many changes to make the text more readable. I am indebted to the great many "plant people" who have shared their knowledge, listened to my stories, and encouraged my outreach. I would be remiss in not acknowledging those who have had the most impact along the way:

Michael Kenton, William and Nancy Bissett, Brightman Logan, David Drylie, Steve Riefler, Rick Joyce, Judith Buhrman, Candace Weller, Marcia Warren, Bruce Turley, and Nancy Desmond. Early reviews of the text were provided by Alexa Wilcox-Huegel and Thomas W. "Bill" Hentges. Cathy Vogelsong provided critical review of the photographs and assisted in selecting the ones to be used. Formatting assistance was provided by my friend and former coworker Wanda Jones. I took most of the photographs, but others contributed significantly. I am indebted to my friends Christina Evans, Shirley Denton, David Williamson, and Roger Hammer for sharing their wonderful photography and allowing all of us to better visualize the connection between wildlife and plants. Finally, I wish to thank the many hundreds of people along the way who have listened to my lectures, asked questions, challenged my opinions, and helped to mold the thoughts and ideas that follow.

Native Plant Landscaping for Florida Wildlife

Planning for Habitat in Landscapes

Florida wildlife species are not declining because of development, but because of the *way* we develop. They do not flee our presence because they can't abide us; they simply cannot make a living within the landscapes that typically replace predevelopment conditions. It is often impossible to replace the habitat elements necessary for a species to survive in our

The Florida fox squirrel is a state-listed species that requires open pinelands. Photo by the author.

The common gray squirrel is found everywhere there are large oaks and other mast-producing trees. Photo by the author.

neighborhoods. Species such as the Florida black bear and Florida panther are never likely to be significantly aided by our landscaping efforts and require a larger-scale approach, but far too many species disappear unnecessarily, and we could do far better for declining species such as gopher tortoise, fox squirrel, and Florida scrub-jay.

The fact that we recognize certain animals as "urban wildlife"—gray squirrels, blue jays, mockingbirds, armadillos, and the like—is the result of frequently seeing them around the places we live and work. Such species, or their close relatives, often thrive in our neighborhoods because they prefer the way we have reshaped nature or at least are well adapted to the species we plant and our typical landscape designs. If we broaden our concept of urban landscape design, we will broaden the diversity of wildlife we regard as "urban."

Over the course of many generations, our Eurocentric aesthetic has radically narrowed our concept of proper landscaping to essentially one design for the landscapes around our homes and places of work. While we might choose different plants in Florida than those of our neighbors in the other 49 states, our landscape plans are nearly identical. The lot is cleared, the home is constructed, and the bare soil is either seeded or sodded with turf grass. Once this is accomplished, a "foundation planting" of shrubs is installed in key locations around the base of the home, a privacy hedge is strategically included to screen the neighbors and a shade tree or two is planted to provide some "interest." Something else is often added for color. Across neighborhoods throughout Florida and the nation, developments spring out of once-diverse natural landscapes, transforming them to a sea of well-manicured turf grass with a couple of shade trees and a line or two of shrubs. We rip the vital organs out of the once-living natural system and replace them with plastic parts that cannot and do not function together.

Native landscapes are living systems, composed of many interacting parts. Take a small patch of native habitat from anywhere and you will find it to be diverse. The ground is carpeted by more than one species of grass, and these are mixed with wildflowers and other herbaceous plants. These ground covers are directly interconnected with the shrubs and trees composing the other layers. The layers are linked. Typical developed landscapes are dysfunctional, because the various parts do not work together. In most cases, they are simply collections of plants. In contrast, native landscapes are communities. There is a big difference between the two.

The typical residential landscape is rather sterile and has very little to offer most Florida wildlife. Photo by the author.

A landscape with a mixture of native plants may attract wildlife, such as this white-eyed vireo, not typically considered "urban wildlife." Photo by David Williamson, with permission.

One of our most important landscape goals is therefore to design for community; to build layers within the landscape that function together and provide the necessary elements of habitat for the wildlife for which we are designing. This may sound complex or restrictive, but it is neither. In reality, it is liberating because it provides so many choices. We can use more of our imagination. Free of the confinement of more traditional designs, we can each select both the design and the plant palette that fits our interests. We do this first by mimicking nature to design the skeleton of a landscape plan.

Natural Florida comprises many different landscapes, each functioning as habitat for the wildlife that live there. If we study native communities, we find some that are open and sunny and others that are deep and shady; those that are relatively "tame" and those that are almost "jungle"-like. In each, we find design elements we can copy to provide habitat. While we may wish to create areas in our landscapes that are dense and impenetrable, it is not a requirement, and there is no need to violate local landscape ordinances or deed restrictions to create wildlife habitat. We can be effective and not arouse the wrath of our neighborhood lawn police. The secret is in selecting plants that work together and provide function. The approach we take is our choice, based on the wildlife for which we are designing and our personal sense of aesthetics.

With each landscape design in nature comes a set of wildlife adapted to it. This interconnected community of plants and wildlife can be purposely designed; in fact, it almost always must be to achieve some level of success. Design by accident is almost always a failure. Careful planning allows us to choose the design that best fits our goals, then we can select the plants we wish to use.

The community we choose as the basis of our design must also work with the growing conditions of our site. Florida is diverse because specific communities develop under specific growing conditions. Small changes in elevation and soil structure have enormous influences on the plant communities in those conditions. Temperature regimes from north to south and the influence of salt spray are also significant. Some communities require deep infertile sands, and others develop only on moist, rich organic soils. No matter what the growing conditions, we find native communities of plants and wildlife adapted to live in them. Work with your site conditions and allow your personal landscape community to develop its own microclimate. Forcing a community on a site lacking the conditions for which it is adapted will almost always lead to disappointment.

Defining Habitat

Understanding that our landscape approach must assemble plants that work well with our site conditions and with each other, and realizing we have a great many plants and landscape designs from which to choose is only part of the equation. We must also understand what habitat means before we can begin the process of selecting plants and incorporating them into a landscape plan. Simply put, habitat is the collection of resources required by each species of wildlife for its survival. In simplest terms, it comprises food, water, and cover. Each species needs to eat and drink and find a place to reside, but it isn't really habitat if the area does

The state and federally threatened Florida scrub-jay requires scrub oaks and open sand to persist in the landscape. Photo by the author.

not provide the type of food, water, and cover that allows the species to grow, mature, successfully reproduce, and persist in time through its off-spring. A box with a food bowl and water bottle is not habitat.

We must also understand that each species has its own habitat requirements that are unique to it. The Florida scrub-jay does not have the same needs in food, water, and cover as its close cousin the blue jay. The former is a state and federally listed species undergoing significant population decline whereas the latter is ubiquitous throughout Florida and the eastern United States. The Florida scrub-jay has very specific habitat needs, and few places in the state are capable of meeting them. In contrast, the blue jay is adaptable. The Florida fox squirrel and the gray squirrel each have very different habitat needs, and the needs of both differ greatly from those of the southern flying squirrel. Over time, each species evolves to use the world a bit differently from every other. It finds a unique niche to exploit, and it adapts to occupy it effectively. Though some species are very adaptable and able to use a wide range of conditions, every species has requirements that must be met in order for it to live within an area. For effective landscape design for wildlife, you must understand the habitat requirements of one or more species in which you are most interested and then design for them.

Your landscape must provide all three components of habitat for each species—food, water, and cover—not just some of them. It is not habitat if something is missing. If you are not providing for a species' survival, it will eventually disappear. Too often, we focus only on food, but the equation has three equal variables and each must be solved.

In many situations, some elements that might be missing from a landscape will be present nearby. If your neighbor shares your interest, for example, some of the food, water, and cover needs for a particular species might be met next door and your landscape won't have the burden of providing everything. Realize, however, that your neighbor's landscape can easily change if his or her interests change or the home is sold to someone who has an entirely different approach. For these reasons, it is always best to rely most on lands you control for developing habitat and then extend your reach to your neighbors. You are in control only of what you own and/or manage.

Finally, you can add the elements of habitat to your landscape either through the landscape itself or by incorporating such "artificial" methods as feeders, houses, and birdbaths. Though the purpose of this book is to guide you through a landscape approach, there is nothing inherently wrong with the "artificial" one *if* what you are adding is the result of a directed approach to incorporate something truly missing and required. Our collective approach to bird feeding, for example, is often ineffective because we provide food that is already abundant and not needed. It's not the feeding of wildlife that is wrong; it's our approach. Many species we routinely feed (e.g., raccoons, gray squirrels, doves) are not limited by a shortage of food. Food is not the missing element in the habitat equation.

Food can sometimes be in short supply. When plants are young, they are likely to produce far less food than when they have matured. While you wait for your plants to grow up and produce seeds, nuts, and fruit, you can augment the food being produced in the landscape by adding the things that are missing. If you have planned well, you will not need this

A bird feeder is effective only when it provides food that would otherwise be missing from the landscape. Photo by David Williamson, with permission.

added food for more than a few years. As a rule, most shrubs should start bearing fruit within a few years, even if you start with smaller one-gallon specimens. Trees will take longer. Medium-sized trees, such as hawthorns (*Crataegus* spp.) and plums (*Prunus* spp.) should start to flower and fruit within 5 years of planting. Large trees, such as oaks (*Quercus* spp.) and hickories (*Carya* spp.), will take 10 years or more.

You may wish to use feeders to supply other foods that you either don't have room to grow or prefer not to grow. Some birds, such as the goldfinch, are especially attracted by thistle seed (as well as Niger seed, which is not a thistle). Though thistles (*Cirsium* spp.) have value as seed producers, a nectar source for many butterflies and other insects, and a larval food source for the caterpillars of the painted lady and little metalmark butterflies, they are an aggressive weed and not a good choice for most home landscapes. It is a lot easier, and often a better landscaping choice, to supply the seed with a feeder than to tie up a portion of your landscape with the plant itself.

The use of feeders can also be extremely effective in supplying food at times of the year when plants are not providing it reliably. Although we strive to make our landscapes reliable, nature may put a kink in our plans. The seasonal use of feeders can mean the difference between maintaining habitat in the landscape year-round or having it fail, especially for species with specialized diets. A good example of this is hummingbirds. Hummingbirds migrate through Florida twice a year. In the fall, they dawdle as they move southward, lingering in areas where nectar sources are abundant. Some remain in extreme south Florida during the winter months if conditions are right, but most skip across the Gulf of Mexico for the tropics. In the spring, these same birds are on a mission to reach their nesting sites, and they are in no mood to take their time. As they hit land after crossing the Gulf of Mexico, they are famished and desperately searching for patches of reliable food. Depending on where you live in Florida, you can take advantage of their situation by supplying sufficient nectar in patches throughout your landscape. If your nectar sources have frozen to the ground by a late frost or you simply have no room to provide food in all the right places, strategically placed feeders can supplement what you have. It may mean the difference between having these amazing animals visit and stay a spell or watching them wing their way over your home.

In all these examples, the underlying concept is that feeders are best used as temporary features of your landscape. If you need to fill in a gap for a few weeks or a few years while the landscape develops and matures, feeders can be effective. The overriding goal, however, is to use the landscape to supply the food that wildlife need. The landscape approach relies on nature to be the provider of habitat and allows everything to eventually reach a natural balance. Supplemental feeding for extended periods is not natural and often causes more problems than it solves. With this approach, everything comes to depend on our continual input, and the house of cards we create implodes as soon as our input is interrupted.

Much the same is true of providing cover with bird and bat boxes. As we discuss more thoroughly a bit later in this book, such boxes are effective in providing only a small element of cover (nesting/roosting cover) for a short time each year; moreover, they do so for only a very small percentage of birds and bats. Bird and bat boxes work only for species that require cavities in which to nest and hide. Most birds and bats do not, and these species will not use a box no matter how well it is built and installed. Even species that might use a box will fail to use one that is improperly designed. If the hole is too large or small, for example, they may ignore it completely, or they may attempt to nest but be more susceptible to predators and lose their young needlessly. Wren houses built "up north" are designed for house wrens, not the Carolina wrens that nest in Florida. House wrens are smaller than Carolina wrens, so northern wren houses (or houses built from those wren house plans) almost always go unused. Bluebird houses can be extremely effective in providing the missing nesting cavity bluebirds require in open pasturelands, but if the hole is a bit too large, European starlings are likely to take over and kill the nestling bluebirds. If you have potential habitat for bluebirds and wish to install houses for them, make sure you use the right plans or purchase the correct house.

As with feeders, nest boxes are effective only when they target specific wildlife and fill a gap where something is missing from the landscape. Many of the common birds in home landscapes (e.g., cardinals, blue jays, mockingbirds, mourning doves) do not nest in cavities and will never use a nest box, but for those birds that require them, nest boxes can make a significant difference. Natural cavities are often lacking in developed landscapes because we are quick to remove dead trees and large dead limbs for safety and liability reasons. I believe that we are often too quick to do this; these dead trees and limbs can be safely left alone for a few years before decay causes them to weaken sufficiently to pose a risk. Dead pines and oaks, for example, often stand for a decade or more in nature before natural forces cause them to fall. During that time, they are likely to produce more insect food and nesting cavities than anything else in the forest.

Houses can be very effective for wildlife, such as these bluebirds, when natural cavities are missing from the landscape. Photo by David Williamson, with permission.

I once took this to heart at a home we purchased that came with a trio of queen palms (*Syagrus romanzoffiana*). In my experience, the non-native queen palm is about as useless a plant for wildlife as one made out of cardboard. Its crown is not dense enough to provide legitimate cover, and the nuts it produces are large and mostly inedible. Wild hogs might consume them, but most of us are not targeting our landscape to benefit those destructive non-native creatures. The two queen palms in the front yard were easy to reach, and I sold them to a company that spaded them out and hauled them off to someone who appreciated them. One of the palms, however, was in the backyard behind a chain-link fence and inaccessible to the tree spade. Faced with the prospect of having to keep this tree that was tying up space something much better might occupy, I cut the top off to kill it. Within a year, the tall dead trunk was alive with cavity-nesting woodpeckers that had excavated a hole near the top. For several years afterward, my dead queen palm was more alive and contributed more to the wildlife habitat of my landscape than it ever had. When it decayed past this point, I took it down. My compromise in leaving a dead tree paid great dividends for several years.

Water features can also be especially important. Few of us live adjacent to a natural water body, but even if we do, providing an additional water feature can produce significant results. While some wildlife get all the water they need from their diet, most need supplemental water for drinking and bathing. Water can be provided to the landscape in many ways, and we will discuss these in greater depth later in this book.

Although water must nearly always be provided by artificial means, food and cover are elements of habitat best provided through the landscape approach. To do so requires development of a plan before we ever purchase a plant or dig a hole in which to plant it. These are issues we must resolve, in order of importance:

1. What type of landscape design will work for me aesthetically and within the community where I reside? Do I want a shady refuge or a mostly sunny, open one? Do I want to change styles in different areas of my property?
2. What types of wildlife am I most interested in supporting with habitat? What are their needs? Can I provide these effectively in my setting and in the landscape style I prefer? What can I compromise to satisfy both conditions?
3. What are my current site conditions? Is my soil coarse and sandy or organic? Is the pH acid or alkaline? Do I contend with salt spray or occasional winter freezes? Can I reasonably alter any features to make room for something that might not naturally perform well under present conditions?
4. What are my realistic plant choices? If I match the site conditions with the needs of my preferred wildlife, which plants remain within this subset of choices that will best achieve my goals?

By setting goals ahead of time, we will avoid the greatest mistake most make: making do with less than the best. There is no reason to settle for second best, nor is there a reason to keep plants that are not doing what we want. We should work with what we have, but we should never keep something that is failing to meet our goals simply because it is growing well and we hate to kill it. If you can, dig it up and give it away if it is wrong for your plan; if not, kill it and replace it. Nature is cruel to plants and animals that are not adapted to a site. Don't be afraid of playing that role.

Selecting Your Landscape Style

As I have tried to convey, developing habitat within a landscape does not restrict us to one style over another. Natural Florida has many habitat styles from which to choose, and each has its own complement of native wildlife. Therefore, we have a great deal of leeway in our selections and should do so after careful and honest consideration of our sense of aesthetics and any restrictions to which our property may be subject. If we are not satisfied with the results, we are not likely to keep them—even if we get some wildlife we were hoping for. It accomplishes little if we finally tire of our landscape and start over with something different. The time we waste by starting over is time that could have been devoted to producing wildlife. It also does no good to bring on the wrath of code enforcement folks for knowingly violating deed restrictions to which we agreed when we bought the property. Our purpose is to create a result that will function as a part of nature and persist over time. We are in hopes that the next owners will view our habitat with pride and value it too.

As we get started, it seems best to come to some understanding of the basic styles we have to work with. Our final landscape needs to be a community where the plants work together to provide food and cover for the wildlife we want to attract. We can do this best by mimicking nature, but within that restriction we have a great many styles to choose from. And, of course, we should not feel confined to using the same style throughout our property. The choice is ours and should be based only on the goals we establish.

As an example of the decision-making process I am referring to, I will use my own experience. When I married my wife, Alexa, I also married her yard. As someone already interested in wildlife and native plants, Alexa had made a great start in adding plants to the few oaks and palmettos the developer had left. Her property is a standard-sized residential lot that was once a well-drained pineland, so those conditions were already established. The live oaks existed as a small grove in the backyard, extending into the yards of two of her neighbors. The palmettos were left in a small cluster in the front. Both these features were things that Alexa valued, and she chose to work with them. Because we love butterflies and wildflowers, we decided to keep the front yard sunny. To do this, we added a few trees and shrubs, but we purposely kept them in patches and left the remaining space more open for native grasses and wildflowers. The backyard was rapidly becoming an oak forest as the oaks grew and filled out. Having the shade meant we had to take a very different approach to this area. Using this shady corner, we decided to add a woody understory of small trees and shrubs, increasing diversity while selecting species native to these conditions. We then added to our woodland by extending it outward. The existing woodland was too small to provide much habitat value. Extending it allowed us to increase both its size and its diversity. Because we already had plenty of oaks, we planted several other kinds of tall trees with different attributes to complement what was already there.

What Alexa and I chose to do was to work with our site and make it our own. We created something that makes sense to us and has provided us with many hours of enjoyment. Although our landscape may not be the same one you would choose, our approach to planning it should be.

Landscapes can remain sunny and open and still provide excellent habitat for wildlife. This is a photo of the author's front yard. Photo by the author.

Shady areas can also provide excellent wildlife habitat, but should have diversity to be most effective. Photo by the author.

Open, Sunny Areas

If you wish to maintain a relatively open and sunny landscape, you can choose to do so and provide for wildlife. As mentioned, the typical residential development is open and sunny, characterized by expansive lawns and widely scattered trees and shrubs. We have come to view this landscape style as "normal," and many of us grow up with a sense of aesthetics that causes us to admire lush green grass and the parklike look this style emulates. The problem is, this approach is also rather foreign: difficult to maintain without large inputs of water, fertilizer, and herbicide, and providing very poor habitat for most species of wildlife. To be honest, some species do manage to eke out a living in these conditions. Nine-banded armadillos flourish in our yards, and eastern moles thrive below ground; mockingbirds find a place to nest most anywhere; and the ubiquitous black racer snake finds plenty of Cuban anoles to prey upon and quiet corners where it can lay low during the daytime. We can create something much better, however, and still adopt a style that is open and sunny. Some of Florida's most interesting and beautiful native communities have this characteristic.

Florida's native sunny plant communities serve well as models for designing better wildlife landscapes. They use essentially the elements of our more traditional landscape approach: grasses, herbaceous flowers, and scattered woody trees and shrubs. If you live in a neighborhood where you have agreed to abide by rather severe landscape restrictions, this basic style might prove the easiest to use as a model for your wildlife landscape.

Of course, making the switch from a traditional style to wildlife habitat requires some major changes in philosophy. For one, the well-manicured turf-grass lawn would be replaced (at least in some locations) by one that relied on native grasses and mowed very infrequently, never to

within 6 inches of the ground. In Florida, that would mean using low-growing bunch grasses, such as wiregrass (*Aristida stricta*) and pinewoods dropseed (*Sporobolus junceus*), mixed with scattered clumps of medium-tall grasses, such as lop-sided indiangrass (*Sorghastrum secundum*), muhly grass (*Muhlenbergia capillipes*), bluestems (*Andropogon* spp.), and little bluestems (*Schizachyrium* spp.). These grasses provide food (seeds, leaves, and insects such as grasshoppers) and cover and the structure necessary to support the herbaceous wildflowers we will add.

Most of us appreciate the beauty of annual and perennial flowers. What we might not fully appreciate is that these species also attract pollinating

Kissimmee Prairie Preserve State Park is an excellent example of the open sunny conditions that naturally occur in Florida dry prairie habitat. Such conditions provide habitat for many types of wildlife. Photo by Christina Evans, with permission.

and foliage-feeding insects that, in turn, help feed songbirds and a host of other wildlife. In our landscape, we will want to introduce herbaceous flowers, preferably native wildflowers, directly into our area of native grasses, not as isolated patches in a formal garden setting. We will also want to select species not only adapted to our growing conditions, but also especially good as nectar sources for pollinators. Others might be selected because they serve as the larval food for butterfly and moth caterpillars. We will use these wildflowers not just for color, but also for the insects they attract and food they provide for songbirds and other wildlife.

If we choose to plant trees and shrubs in this area, we will need to avoid those that produce too much shade. Broadleaf hardwoods, such as oaks and maples, will not allow sufficient sunlight through their canopies to keep a grassland understory alive. Pines are especially good at filtering light to reduce its intensity while letting enough in. Any of our native pines would be good choices in this setting, but the best might be longleaf and slash pine (*Pinus palustris* and *P. elliottii*, respectively). A few deciduous trees with narrow crowns or thin open branches can also work. Good choices here would be turkey and bluejack oaks (*Quercus laevigata* and *Q. incana*, respectively).

Muhly grass is just one example of a Florida native grass with aesthetic beauty and habitat value. Photo by the author.

Wildflowers such as this native aster provide far better habitat value than most cultivated non-natives. Photo by the author.

Adopting this approach would not necessarily require us to use it everywhere. There may be good reason to have some turf-grass lawn if you need places to entertain or spots to throw a baseball, for example, but most of us have large tracts of lawn that provide nothing but work and expense. Rid yourself of this burden and create habitat in its place.

Privacy Areas

Most of us are not willing to completely give up the standard privacy hedge or foundation planting. Typical residential landscapes have planted areas that provide these functions. Sometimes, they are at the outside perimeters of the property and serve to block the view of the neighbors, or they are used around the foundation to break up the starkness of a straight wall. At other times, we create patches of color to break up the monotony of the open lawn. Regardless of why we have them, most provide little function other than aesthetics.

Most habitats in nature also have patches of dense vegetation, and we can look to these for guidance in creating habitat for wildlife. Perhaps the foremost difference between traditional privacy plantings and nature is that nature rarely creates monocultures. We would take a huge leap forward if we did the same in our landscapes. The next leap, and the one that seals the deal, would be selecting plants based on function instead of aesthetics, availability, or whatever the neighbors have next door.

Mixing multiple species in a privacy hedge or foundation planting offers a broader spectrum of food and cover than a single species ever will. This is true whether you choose to prune these areas occasionally or not. Our tendency to use single species for hedges and plantings has no rational basis and significantly limits the plantings from providing meaningful wildlife habitat.

Mixing native shrubs greatly increases their overall habitat value and can be far more aesthetically interesting. Photo by the author.

Florida's native flame azalea provides effective color in the native plant understory. Colorful natives can be substituted for the more commonly used non-native species and increase habitat value at the same time. Photo by the author.

The same is true of plantings designed to provide color, for example, the traditional azalea bed under the shade tree. Color plantings do not have to be abandoned in the wildlife landscape, but the plants we use must provide more than color. Florida is blessed with many colorful flowering trees and shrubs besides azaleas. Incorporating them into landscapes provides habitat without sacrificing beauty.

This does not mean we cannot use the azalea bed in our landscape plans; just that we understand the limitations of such plantings and compensate for them elsewhere. If we choose something strictly for aesthetics, we must work extra hard elsewhere to create meaningful habitat.

Shady Areas

Many of us also have areas shaded by large canopy trees such as oaks. Even if we don't, we may wish to create such an area of cool, shady conditions everybody wants in the heat of summer. Shade, by itself, has value. The problem with most shady areas in the traditional landscape is that shade is the only thing being considered. Dense shade under a live oak (*Quercus virginiana*) is useless if all we shade is turf grass. Too often, we plant shade trees in the middle of a yard with no real sense of what that will mean once the tree has matured. In those situations, we are left with a bare patch in the lawn where nothing seems to grow. We have created a problem area instead of valuable habitat.

Turf grasses do not grow well in shade. No matter what the ads tell you, they don't perform well in this condition. So, once again, we look to nature for habitats that are shady to identify plants that perform in these conditions.

In Florida, shady forested areas are normally referred to as hammocks. Coastal hammocks develop near the coastlines with plants adapted to salt

A live oak has shaded the lawn grass and made the area beneath it ugly and useless to wildlife. Planting shade-tolerant ground covers would resolve this problem. Photo by the author.

A native hammock understory is both diverse and interesting. Photo by the author.

spray. Hydric hammocks develop in areas that frequently flood, and xeric hammocks form on droughty soils that never flood. Hammock forests vary from north to south Florida, from coastal areas to inland ones, and under all varieties of soil and moisture regimes. What ties them together is that all include canopy trees shading the understory, and the understory plants are well adapted to these conditions.

If we inherit shade in our landscape, or desire to create it, we need to look at these systems for guidance on wildlife habitat. The first step is to look at the canopy. Hammock canopies are not composed of only one species. Often, they contain a great many, but our traditional approach is to use very few. Too often, the shade around our homes is the product of fast-growing non-natives that perform their task quickly but are weak and short lived. If our landscapes include native shade trees, they are nearly always either live or laurel oak (*Quercus laurifolia*), southern magnolia (*Magnolia grandiflora*), or red maple (*Acer rubrum*). While these trees have their value in the landscape, a native hammock might have all four, plus others that are rarely purposely planted. If you have the space and the desire to create a forest in your home landscape, add diversity to the canopy.

What often confounds people, however, is what to do in shady places. It seems we run out of ideas if grass won't grow there. Hammocks have very few grasses in their understory, and these do not perform the same functions as turf grasses in a lawn. Basket grass (*Oplismenus hirtellus*), for example, is a ground-hugging species that spreads rapidly but cannot withstand heavy foot traffic. Inland river oats (*Chasmanthium laxum*) is poorly adapted to sites that are not moist and is really useful only as an accent grass because of its height.

Because they are shady, hammocks normally also have few colorful wildflowers in their understory. Those hammocks that do are deciduous in the winter and contain flowers, such as violets (*Viola* spp.), that bloom in the spring before the canopy leafs out. Plant these species at the outer edges of a hammock for best results and visibility.

A hammock understory comprises mostly perennials such as ferns and woody shrubs such as coffees (*Psychotria* spp.). While ferns are hardly colorful, their form and texture can lend a subtle beauty to the landscape. Florida is home to more than 100 native ferns and a good number of other non-native species that are not aggressive nuisances. Mix several species together, depending on your growing conditions, and add structure with woody species adapted to low light.

The other important feature of the hammock understory is leaf litter. While we too often use mulches only for aesthetic purposes and want the types that don't easily decay, a hammock develops a rich topsoil layer as its natural mulch decays. It is this rich surface layer that often contains the most life in a hammock forest. The great diversity of invertebrates (e.g., worms and insects) creates the foundation of this food web and feeds the higher organisms. If you visit a natural hammock, try to see where all the

A hammock understory supports a variety of ferns and other shade-tolerant plants. The leaf litter enriches the soil and provides ideal conditions for earthworms and other invertebrates. Photo by the author.

activity is. It's in the upper canopy, where light allows many more species of insects to exist, and on the forest floor, where decaying leaf litter attracts the rest. The energy driving this system is either streaming in as sunlight or being released from decaying leaf litter that stored the sunlight the year before.

Hammocks often have a rich subcanopy: a layer of small trees and shrubs adapted to low light that often bloom in the early spring when the canopy is sparsest. By using a mixture of such plants, you can create springtime color and wildlife food and cover.

Through this exercise, I have hopefully provided a starting point for your landscape plan. We will explore this in much greater detail later in this book. Realize that you are free to take whatever approach you need to meet your goals. Your creativity should be held at bay only by the restrictions of your property and the needs of the wildlife you want to attract. It is those needs that we will discuss next.

Selecting Wildlife

Once you have made decisions regarding landscape style, it is time to incorporate them into the wildlife considerations you also need to make. In truth, both decisions should be made together, and this is where your sense of compromise comes into play. Some wildlife require the dense and shady conditions of a hammock-type community, while others need something more open and sunny. You will need to take some time in the beginning to purposefully decide the types of wildlife you want in your landscape and then take the time to get to know their specific habitat requirements. Only by understanding their diet and their cover needs can you begin to compose your plant list and landscape plan.

Tables 1.1–1.3 list the food and cover requirements of the most common wildlife you might wish to include in your plan. The list does not include butterflies as so many books are available on butterfly gardening in Florida. Should you wish to target more of your landscape for these species, consult these specialty books for information on their habitat needs. I have included some of my favorites in the resource section at the end of this book. The list of wildlife in the tables is not meant to be exhaustive, nor is it meant to be limiting. Your geographic or local conditions might allow you to create habitat for species most of us could not plan for. Just because something is not on the list does not mean you can't target your approach for it. Ultimately, your list must be yours. Take the time to do some research on the wildlife species in which you are most interested, including what they require for food and cover. Many books are available with that information, and I have included a list of some of the best at the end of this book. The time you take at the beginning will be rewarded later in results.

In developing your wildlife list, you must first and foremost be realistic. You cannot provide for wildlife that are not resident in your region of Florida, and you will not be successful if you cannot provide all the elements of habitat in the area you are landscaping. Beware of lists, for

Table 1.1. Common Florida Reptiles and Amphibians and Their Habitat Needs

Common Name	Diet	Cover Needs	Comments
Tree frogs	Insects, other invertebrates	Breed in shallow wetlands and ponds. Adults most common in pinelands and brushy areas	Cuban tree frogs should not be encouraged as they displace smaller native species
Anoles	Insects, other invertebrates	Occur in wide variety of open and wooded habitats; brown anoles especially common around homes in developed landscapes	Native anole changes color from green to light brown, far less common in urban and suburban landscapes than brown or Cuban anole
Southern toad/ Oak toad	Insects, other invertebrates	Breeds in shallow wetlands and ponds; adults in various upland habitats	Larger southern toad widely distributed, often encountered around developed landscapes; small oak toad most common in pinelands, open oak forests
Box turtle	Insects, other invertebrates, fruit, carrion	Box turtles prefer moist woodlands, brushy grasslands	Juvenile box turtles feed far more on worms, snails, other invertebrates than adults
Gopher tortoise	Sunny uplands with well-drained soils	Grasses, herbaceous plants, fruits	Gopher tortoises protected by state law, cannot be handled or kept as pets
Black racer	Insects, lizards, other small animals; juveniles eat mostly insects, small lizards; adults may eat small mammals, birds.	Occurs nearly everywhere; hides in dense vegetation, brush piles	Perhaps most common snake in developed landscapes in Florida

Table 1.2 Common Florida Mammals and Their Habitat Needs

Common Name	Diet	Cover Needs	Comments
White-tailed deer	Browsers; new growth of woody plants year-round; acorns in fall; herbaceous plants in spring, summer	Uses wide variety of wooded habitats; hides in thickets during day; fawns generally reared in brushy areas	Make little use of grasses as forage; can be serious pest of ornamentals
Gray squirrel	Nuts and acorns, seeds, occasional soft fruit; may eat bulbs, vegetation	Hardwood forests, urban landscapes dominated by oaks; builds leafy nests in trees	Extremely common in developed landscapes
Fox squirrel	Pine seeds, acorns, nuts, soft fruit; may eat bulbs	Open pinelands with scattered oaks; builds leafy nests in trees	Often forages on the ground
Flying squirrel	Nuts and acorns, berries, insects	Hardwood forests and pinelands; nests in cavities	May use a nest box; active mostly at night
Deer mouse	Acorns, nuts, seeds, soft fruit, insects	Occurs in variety of woodland habitats; builds nests in cavities, hollow structures	Rarely a house pest; prefers living outdoors
Rabbits (Cottontail/ Marsh)	Legumes, grasses, broad-leaved herbaceous plants	Cottontails common in brushy areas, open forests; marsh rabbits common in densely vegetated marshes, wetland edges	Both species largely nocturnal, create nests in dense grassy areas
Bats	Night-flying insects, especially moths and beetles	Yellow, red, and Seminole commonly roost in small groups in tops of trees; Brazilian free-tailed, Florida mastiff, and brown in cavities; gray and Indiana in caves	Cavity-roosting species may also use bat boxes; no bat species feeds on mosquitoes to any significant extent

continued

Common Name	Diet	Cover Needs	Comments
Raccoon	Wide range of plant and animal material	Nests in cavities in wide variety of natural and manmade structures	Do not encourage raccoons by feeding them directly; raccoons common carriers of rabies
Opossum	Nearly every type of animal and vegetable food	Lives virtually anywhere with trees; normally nests in trees, may occupy attics, other buildings	Opossums are marsupials, carry young offspring in pouches
Gray fox	Rabbits, rodents, other animal food, also fruit	May live in virtually every upland habitat type; dens underground burrows or hollow logs	Can climb trees in pursuit of prey or to escape
Coyote	Mostly small mammals; nearly everything from fruit to carrion and garbage	Generally builds underground dens but will use nearly any concealed structure or culvert; occupies nearly every habitat type	Coyotes rapidly increasing in developed parts of Florida and can become a nuisance; keep pets and pet food indoors

Table 1.3. Common Florida Birds and Their Habitat Needs

Common Name	Residency Status	Nesting Season Diet	Fall/Winter Diet	Nesting Habitat	Winter Habitat	General Comments
Wading birds (Egrets, Herons, and Ibis)	Resident	Fish, frogs, reptiles, small mammals	Same	In colonies near water or on islands in small trees and dense shrubs	Prefers shallow water habitats, not too thickly vegetated	Herons and egrets may nest in mixed species colonies; many species forage in suburban yards for lizards, snakes, and insects
Hawks and Eagles	Most common species in developed landscapes in Florida are resident, including red-shouldered hawk, red-tailed hawk, osprey, American bald eagle, kestrel, Cooper's hawk. Non-resident hawks common in winter include sharp-shinned hawk, Northern harrier	Most: other birds and small mammals; osprey and bald eagles: mostly fish; bald eagles also eat wide variety of mammals, carrion	Same	Canopies of mature trees; use nest platforms.	Generally spot prey visually and prefer to hunt in sparsely wooded areas, over open fields and wetlands; red-shouldered hawks most common in and around forested wetlands	Many hawks attracted to birds at bird feeders, especially ground and platform feeders that attract non-native rock pigeons and Eurasian collared doves

Screech owl	Resident	Mostly nocturnal insects, lizards, small rodents	Same	Nest in cavities; use nest boxes	Common in a wide variety of habitats, including suburban landscapes	Population restricted by availability of cavities; nest boxes often quickly occupied if established by early winter
Barred owl	Resident	Small mammals, birds, large insects	Same	Canopy of mature trees or in cavities; may use nest boxes	Mostly in and near forested wetlands	The species most often called a "hoot" owl
Turkey	Resident	Breeding season diet mostly insects	Acorns, fruits, wide variety of seeds	Nests constructed on the ground in open, brushy fields	Uses a wide variety of habitats during the year, prefers open woodlands and fields	Not likely to occur in developed landscapes
Bobwhite quail	Resident	Beetles and other insects especially important in spring and early summer	Mainly acorns, seeds, fruits; invertebrates still important	Nests constructed on the ground in dense grass and brush	In Florida, prefer pinelands with open understory and brushy agricultural fields	Not likely to occur in developed landscapes
Mourning dove	Resident	Seeds	Seeds	Lower branches of small trees and shrubs, sometimes on manmade structures	Prefers open lands and open woodlands; common resident of urban and suburban landscapes	May nest nearly year-round and up to 3 times; young fed partially digested seeds (crop milk), regurgitated from the crops of parents

continued

Common Name	Residency Status	Nesting Season Diet	Fall/Winter Diet	Nesting Habitat	Winter Habitat	General Comments
Ground dove	Resident	Seeds	Seeds	Nests constructed on the ground or near the ground in lower branches of woody plants.	Open fields and woodlands. Not often found in developed landscapes.	May nest nearly year-round, up to 4 times; populations generally decreasing statewide.
Woodpeckers	Resident, except yellow-bellied sapsucker, a winter resident only Species most common to developed landscapes are downy and red-bellied woodpeckers, Northern flicker	Insects	Insects; most also eat a variety of acorns, fruit, seeds; these plant foods especially important to red-bellied woodpecker	Cavities in live and dead trees; some species infrequently use nest boxes	Most species common in open woodlands and agricultural areas with widely spaced trees—red-headed woodpeckers mostly in open sandy pinelands; pileated woodpeckers mostly in forested wetlands	Most woodpeckers can reside in developed landscapes given the right habitat conditions
Ruby-throated hummingbird	Nesting northern half of Florida; migratory southern half	Nectar from tubular flowers; some tiny insects	Same	Thin lower branches of trees and shrubs, often near water	Prefers open habitats with abundant nectar sources	Feeders can greatly supplement flower nectar sources; highly territorial; locate feeders in different areas of the landscape; never use honey; change feeder solution often during hot summer months

Chuckwill's widow	Nesting	Nocturnal insects captured in flight	N/A	Builds nest on the ground in open woodlands	Open hardwood and pineland forests	May reside in developed landscapes where woodlots are still present
Common nighthawk	Breeding	Nocturnal insects captured in flight	N/A	Eggs laid on the ground without a nest	Wide variety of open habitats	A closely related species, the Antillean nighthawk, found only in extreme south Florida
Chimney swift	Breeding	Insects captured in flight	N/A	Nests constructed with mud and attached to the inside of natural cavities, chimneys, other manmade structures	Wide variety of open habitats	Nest in colonies; most active in early morning and at dusk

continued

Common Name	Residency Status	Nesting Season Diet	Fall/Winter Diet	Nesting Habitat	Winter Habitat	General Comments
Swallows	Several swallows nest in Florida, but only rough-winged swallow is resident; tree and bank swallows common winter residents but do not nest here	Insects captured in flight	Mostly insects; fruit, especially wax myrtle berries	Most attach mud nests to the sides of cavities and manmade structures, including chimneys, house porches, undersides of bridges; some species, particularly rough-winged swallows, also nest in cavities in the banks of streams and rivers	Prefer open habitats with few trees	Sensitive to the presence of forested lands and rarely use areas where trees are common; nest in colonies
Purple martin	Breeding	Insects captured in flight	N/A	Natural and manmade cavities in open habitats, usually near water; will use specially designed martin houses or gourds	Require open habitat and prefer foraging over open water and in open areas adjacent to lakes and ponds	Purple martins nest in colonies; do not use martin houses made of aluminum or other metals in Florida; make sure martin houses are cleaned and installed by mid-February each year or unlikely to be used

Great crested flycatcher	Breeding	Insects, especially moths, caterpillars; some fruits	N/A	Tree canopy	Mixed woodlands	Some birds winter in extreme south Florida
Blue jay	Resident	Insects, small birds, lizards; some fruits	Acorns, nuts, fruits; less animal food	Tree canopy	Mixed forests and open lands with mature mast-producing trees	A common bird of developed landscapes where oaks and other mast-producing trees are planted as shade trees; commonly attracted to feeders
Florida scrub-jay	Resident	Insects, lizards, other small animals; some fruits	Acorns of scrub oaks extremely important; some fruits	Dense foliage of scrub oaks and other woody plants 6–9 feet above ground	Scrub and scrubby flatwoods with extensive open sand for burying acorns	Unlike the common blue jay, the Florida scrub-jay is extremely habitat sensitive and declining rapidly because of habitat loss Preserving scrub in the landscape where they are present would preserve scrub-jays post-development.

continued

Common Name	Residency Status	Nesting Season Diet	Fall/Winter Diet	Nesting Habitat	Winter Habitat	General Comments
Tufted titmouse	Resident	Caterpillars and other insects especially important; some fruits and seeds	Seeds and fruits; insects still important	Nests in cavities; will use nest boxes	Common in a wide variety of woodland habitats	Limited by availability of suitable cavities for nesting; nest boxes can be especially important for attracting them to a landscape
Carolina chickadee	Resident	Similar to tufted titmouse, caterpillars and small insects in breeding season; some small seeds	Mostly insects; small seeds and fruits	Nests in cavities; may use a bird house	Resident to a wide variety of wooded habitats	Commonly associated with titmice, have similar habits and requirements; often attracted to bird feeders but diet mostly insects
Nuthatches	White-breasted and brown-headed nuthatch resident to north Florida, rarer farther south	Insects gleaned from bark of pines, other trees	Acorns and other mast important to white-breasted nuthatches; pine and other small seeds important to brown-headed nuthatches; insects	Both species are cavity nesters, but unlikely to use nest boxes	White-breasted nuthatches found in a variety of woodland habitats; brown-headed nuthatches prefer open pinelands	Both species have declined sharply in recent years

Northern mockingbird	Resident	Mostly insects, some small fruits	Mostly small fruits and berries, some insects	Builds its own nest 6–10 feet above ground in dense trees and shrubs	Edges and open woodlands and fields with widely spaced trees	One of the most common birds in suburban Florida
Gray catbird	Winter resident; a few may nest in extreme north Florida	Insects, some small fruits	Berries and other soft fruits, some insects	Builds its own nest in dense shrubs and thickets	Edges and open woodlands, often hiding in thickets of denser cover	Catbirds extremely common winter residents, but most comfortable in locations that offer some dense hiding cover
Brown thrasher	Resident	Wide variety of insects, some berries, small fruits	Wide variety of fruits, seeds, small nuts; insects	Builds its own nest 6–10 off the ground in dense shrubs or trees	Prefers open woodlands and grasslands with patches of dense woody cover	A common bird of developed landscapes
Carolina wren	Resident	Mostly invertebrates, especially ants, bees, spiders, caterpillars	Mostly invertebrates; rarely small berries and seeds	Cavities and nest boxes in dense cover.	Prefers thickets in a wide variety of woodlands and open habitats	One of the most common birds in Florida and one of the likeliest to use a nest box; be careful not to use a box designed for the smaller northern house wren

continued

Common Name	Residency Status	Nesting Season Diet	Fall/Winter Diet	Nesting Habitat	Winter Habitat	General Comments
Thrushes	Hermit and wood thrushes mostly winter residents; wood thrush may nest occasionally in north Florida; other thrushes present only during spring and fall migration	Wood thrush mostly insects, some small fruits	All: mixed diet of insects and small fruits and berries	Wood thrush builds own nest in dense shrubs	All: woodland habitats with open areas on the ground for foraging	Thrushes not common in most residential landscapes, but can be found when habitat conditions are favorable
American robin	Winter resident	N/A	In Florida, mostly soft berries, other fruits; some insects	N/A	Although robins are a species of thrush, they prefer open woodlands and fields with some woody cover for hiding and roosting	Often occur in large flocks in winter and move around widely as they strip local trees and shrubs of fruits
Eastern bluebird	Resident	Mostly insects	Mostly soft fruits, berries; some insects	Natural cavities and nest boxes.	Open woodlands and agricultural areas with widely spaced trees	Declining and rare in suburban landscapes; require wide-open habitats not often found in developed areas
Blue-gray gnatcatcher	Resident	Small insects gleaned from foliage and twigs of trees and shrubs	Same	Nests they construct in outer branches of mature trees	A variety of woodlands	A tiny active bird frequently seen foraging with titmice and chickadees

Cedar waxwing	Winter resident	N/A	Like the American robin, mostly soft fruits, berries; some insects	N/A	Like the American robin, uses a wide variety of open woodlands and open areas with dense woody cover for roosting	Often seen here in large flocks or in flocks mixed with robins; usually arrive in areas where large fruit crops are present, strip the fruit in a few days and move on
Vireos	Most nest in Florida; only blue-headed vireo strictly migratory to the state; most nesting vireos are resident, but red-eyed and black-whiskered migrate to the tropics in winter	Mostly insects, some small fruits and seeds	Same	Build their own nests in tree canopies	Woodlands	Common in canopies of trees in a wide variety of habitats; some species may nest in woodlots or large woody areas in developed landscapes
Warblers—Nesting						
Prothonotary	Nesting, migrates to the tropics in winter	Insects	N/A	Natural cavities and sometimes nest boxes in forested wetland trees	Forested wetlands	Most common to extensive forested wetlands

continued

Common Name	Residency Status	Nesting Season Diet	Fall/Winter Diet	Nesting Habitat	Winter Habitat	General Comments
Northern parula	Nesting, migrates to the tropics in winter	Insects gleaned from foliage and branches of mature trees	N/A	Builds own nest in canopy of mature trees	Woodlands	Common nesting warbler in much of Florida
Yellow-throated	Resident to north Florida, winter resident elsewhere	Insects	Insects	Builds own nest in canopy of mature trees	Mixed pine and hardwood forests, open deciduous forests	Often observed singly in mixed flocks of insectivorous songbirds
Common yellowthroat	Resident	Insects	Insects	Builds own nest just above ground in dense vegetation	Mixed woodlands, shrubby marshes, brushy open areas	Very common warbler in dense brushy habitats
Prairie	Nesting, migrates to the tropics in winter	Insects	N/A	Builds own nest in dense mangroves, sometimes in dense shrubs	Not a bird of open areas; prefers shrubby habitats	A boldly marked warbler; can be attracted to developed landscapes given the right conditions
Pine	Resident	Mostly insects captured on the wing or gleaned from bark and foliage of mature trees	Insects, seeds, variety of small fruits and berries	Builds own nest, often in canopies of mature pines	Variety of open woodlands, especially those with pines	Relatively common Florida warbler

Warblers—Winter Residents				
Yellow-rumped	Winter resident	N/A	Relies on wide variety of small fruit, especially those of wax myrtle; insects	Wide variety of open woodlands and open habitats with some brushy cover	Common in large flocks throughout Florida and in suburban landscapes
Palm	Winter resident	N/A	Mostly insects gleaned from understory vegetation; seeds	Wide variety of open brushy and woody habitats, including suburban areas	Very common winter warbler; often seen in flocks feeding on the ground; distinguished by tail-bobbing behavior
Black-and-white	Winter resident	N/A	Insects gleaned from bark of limbs and trunks	Common winter resident of forested areas and open woodlands	Commonly seen in mixed feeding flocks, working up and down trunks and branches
Ovenbird	Winter resident	N/A	Insects gleaned from leaf litter; some small fruits and seeds	Shady forest understory	A very secretive bird of woodland understory

continued

Common Name	Residency Status	Nesting Season Diet	Fall/Winter Diet	Nesting Habitat	Winter Habitat	General Comments
Warblers—Migratory Only						
All other warblers	Migratory	N/A	Insects	N/A	Most prefer wooded habitats; appropriate suburban landscapes can strongly attract these species during migration, but most continue migration within 24 hours of arrival	
Grackles and Blackbirds	Red-winged blackbird, boat-tailed and common grackles are common and resident; Brewer's, rusty, and yellow-headed blackbirds are migratory and infrequent	Insects especially important; some seeds and grains	Seeds and grains especially important; some insects and other small animals	Builds own nest several feet above ground in dense shrubby or marshy habitats	Often associated with agricultural lands and developed areas, open marshes and fields	Blackbirds and grackles often considered nuisance birds; cause damage to agricultural areas
Eastern meadowlark	Resident	Mostly insects, especially grasshoppers, crickets, caterpillars	Mostly insects; some seeds and grains	Grasslands	Open grasslands, pastures, and brushlands with few trees	Unlikely to be attracted to developed landscapes

Northern oriole	Winter resident	N/A	Wide variety of insects, seeds, small fruit	N/A	Open woodlands, open habitats with scattered trees, agricultural lands	Sometimes attracted to sliced oranges placed on feeding stations
Summer tanager	Nesting	Insects, especially caterpillars and beetles; small fruits	N/A	Builds own nest in canopy of mature trees	Woodlands	Most likely encountered in expansive woodlands
Northern cardinal	Resident	Insects important when feeding nestlings; seeds and small fruit at other times	Seeds, small fruits	Builds own nest 4–8 feet above ground in dense shrubs, sometimes small trees	Wide variety of forested and open habitats	One of the most common residents of developed landscapes
Blue grosbeak	Nesting, north Florida to south-central Florida	Insects, seeds, grains	N/A	Builds own nest 4–8 feet above ground in dense shrubs or small trees	Open woodlands, brushy agricultural areas	Unlikely to be attracted to developed landscapes
Indigo bunting	Nesting, north Florida; migrant elsewhere; a few may overwinter in southern half of state	Some insects during nesting season; seeds and some small fruits	Mostly seeds and small fruits	Builds own nest near the ground in dense shrubs	Open woodlands, brushy areas, field edges	Not uncommon in brushy habitats near woodlands and agricultural areas

continued

Common Name	Residency Status	Nesting Season Diet	Fall/Winter Diet	Nesting Habitat	Winter Habitat	General Comments
House finch	Winter resident; becoming established as a resident breeding bird in parts of the state	Mostly seeds, some insects and small fruits	Seeds, some insects and small fruits	Ledges, manmade and natural cavities, dense shrubs	Open habitats; well adapted to suburban landscapes	Becoming more common in developed landscapes
American goldfinch	Winter resident	N/A	Mostly seeds, some insects	N/A	Open brushy fields, open woodlands, agricultural areas	Common in large flocks in winter
Eastern towhee	Resident	Insects mostly gleaned from leaf litter; some small fruits	Same; fruits and seeds more important after nesting season	Builds own nest near the ground in dense palmettos and other shrubs	Pinelands and brushlands with dense woody midcanopy	Common, but rather secretive; needs dense understory
Sparrows	Most sparrows in Florida winter residents that nest farther north; resident sparrows: Bachman's, seaside, and Florida grasshopper, are rare habitat specialists, unlikely to occur in developed landscapes	N/A—resident species feed extensively on insects in nesting season	Weed and grass seeds especially important; some insects	N/A—resident species nest near the ground in dense woody vegetation or in grasses on the ground	Migratory species most abundant in old fields and brushy edges; Bachman's sparrow prefers open dry pinelands with widely spaced trees; seaside sparrow in coastal marshes; Florida grasshopper sparrow in dry prairie and pasturelands with few woody species	The common English or House sparrow is not a true sparrow and is a non-native species that should not be encouraged; most true sparrows prefer brushy edges and overgrown fields

An atala butterfly and its host plant, Florida coontie (*Zamia pumila*). Although coonties grow statewide, the atala requires the more tropical conditions found only in extreme south Florida. Photo by the author.

example, that tell only part of the story. Some species simply will never reside in your part of Florida, and landscaping your property for them would be a waste of time. White-crowned pigeons and Schaus swallowtails are resident to extreme south Florida, whereas red-spotted purple butterflies and nuthatches are not.

Do not design your landscape for species that require far more room than you can provide or conditions you cannot create. Understand the limitations of the setting you are landscaping. If you are surrounded by woodland, for example, you might ultimately be able to provide suitable conditions for songbirds that require expansive forest; otherwise, you must be content with species satisfied with smaller woodland patches, or migratory species that will use it for a few days on their way north or south. If you have a standard lot and your neighbors have a standard landscape, you will have to work with the area you have. You can do a great deal with a standard lot, but there will be certain wildlife whose needs you will never be able to satisfy in that setting.

Come to an understanding of the seasons when the wildlife might be present. Some, such as northern cardinals, Carolina wrens, and northern mockingbirds are resident year-round. You will need to provide habitat these species can use all twelve months of the year. Others are resident only part of the year, for example, during the winter months or for spring/summer breeding season. Many of our most interesting birds fall into these categories. Just because they are here for only part of the year does not mean you should ignore them in your planning; only that your landscape plan must meet their habitat needs only during the months of their stay. Still others are migrants and may be here for only a short time as they pass through to other places. If it is important to you that these species stop in your yard on their way through town, add their habitat needs to your landscape design.

As you plan for wildlife, pay special attention to whether their habitat needs might change with the seasons. Many species change their diet during the course of the year. A good example is the yellow-rumped warbler, or what used to be called the myrtle warbler. As is true of other warblers, the yellow-rumped warbler needs a steady diet of small insects during the breeding and nesting season, but it spends this part of its life "up north," so that does not concern us here in Florida. When it arrives here in late fall, the yellow-rumped warbler is primarily a fruit-eating bird, specializing in the ripe fruit of wax myrtles. If your landscape is producing wax myrtle fruit, you most certainly will be visited by this species. If it also meets its cover requirements, you may have them all winter.

Cover needs also change with the seasons. Nesting cover may be very different from wintering cover. Birds that require one type to successfully nest may need something different when nesting is completed. Mammals, reptiles, butterflies, and other wildlife often have similar habitat requirements throughout the year, but those that either hibernate or spend the winter in some sort of resting phase may have specialized requirements that are different from what they need the rest of the year. You need to provide for the cover requirements of each species for the time of year they are present.

Finally, don't be overwhelmed or try to do too much. Take on what you can do well. If you take on too much, you may very well end up less

During the winter months, the yellow-rumped warbler feeds extensively on the fruit of wax myrtles. Photo by David Williamson, with permission.

successful than your neighbor who started out with less ambitious goals. Especially if you are a rather novice gardener, or new to native plants, tackle your landscape in pieces. Lay out your overall plan up front, but don't try to landscape it all at one time. Start with the areas of your landscape that might take the longest time to develop—a woodland, for example. Get it established and then take on the next project. And, most importantly, do not be afraid to modify your plans as you go. You may find that something is simply not going to work or that something else might work better. Stay open to new ideas and revisions that make sense, but keep your underlying goals.

Understanding Your Existing Conditions

Before you can start to make plant choices, you must effectively evaluate your particular conditions. This might seem almost too obvious, but it is extremely important. Most of us, at one time or another, have tried to force a plant into a landscape for which it was not adapted. We have seen a plant that intrigued us and we wanted it. Either we knew up front that it would not work well, or we purchased it in ignorance of what it needed and decided that we would figure out where to put it later. Such an approach to landscaping just doesn't work. Landscaping for wildlife is not about selecting plants because we like them and then making them work, but about selecting plants that will fulfill our landscaping goals and letting them work for us. While we are doing that, we will also be looking at aesthetics and selecting plants that appeal to us, but we will like them more for their function than their aesthetic qualities.

Understanding your growing conditions and matching plants to what you have is absolutely crucial to your ultimate success. Sometimes you can change those conditions by creating new microclimates. You do this when you shade an area that was formerly sunny. You can alter your soil fertility somewhat by adding compost and mulch and then maintaining it. You can increase soil moisture levels by directing rainwater from your roof to localized areas of your yard. But, in the long term, we are all given a set of soil and moisture conditions when we purchase our property, and it is best to work with those conditions. Straying too far afield will likely cause our plants to fail and our habitat to crash and burn.

Although this book is devoted to the use of native plants, do not be fooled into thinking that native plants are any more adapted to your site than non-native ones. The simple fact that a plant grows naturally in Florida does not mean that it will grow naturally in your yard. Florida has one of the most diverse palettes of native plants in the nation because it has so many species that require unique conditions. It's the diversity of growing conditions statewide that ensures a diversity of native plants. Your yard is unlikely to have much diversity in growing conditions, so you will have to work with the plants adapted to it.

Although many plants tolerate a broad range of conditions, many others do not. We should use the specialized species too, but with some forethought. Do not try to force a plant of the Florida scrub into a soil that isn't coarse sand, and do not put a moist hammock species into a sunny spot in typical sandy conditions unless it is proven to be one of the adaptable species.

Many Florida soils are sandy, but not all sandy soils are alike. If you have gardened up north, you likely did so in much different soil conditions. Far too often, we bring our past gardening knowledge to Florida and it gets in our way. There is nothing wrong with sand for growing plants. Thousands of beautiful native species have done just fine here for millennia. Our prejudice for the rich organic soils of the Midwest or the red clay soils of other southern states will ultimately frustrate our gardening efforts here.

You cannot effectively amend your soil. Digging a hole and refilling it with some type of bagged topsoil from somewhere else may look sensible, but it will have no lasting impact on your landscape. The roots of your plant will eventually reach out of that little pocket of amended soil, and the organics you have added will eventually decompose. Over time, your plant will once again be rooted in the soil with which you started. Your goal is to create a community of plants that will persist and function together. This will happen effectively only if you choose plants to start with that thrive in the growing conditions you have.

Many sands have lower fertility than the higher organic soils of elsewhere. That does not mean that the plants that grow in them require fertilizer to thrive. If you have selected wisely and chosen native species that naturally grow in these conditions, your plants will get all the nutrients they need from the soil you already have. Providing additional fertilizer can often be harmful instead of helpful when you have a native landscape. Pulses of increased nutrients can force your plants to respond with pulses of growth. Far too often, this unnatural growth is both weak and susceptible to increased insect and disease damage. Instead of providing a benefit, you are opening your plants to a host of problems to which they are ill adapted.

Sands also allow water to percolate more rapidly and for air exchange to occur around roots. Many of our native plants require this combination of moisture and "openness" around their roots and will die if they do not get it. Holding too much moisture too tightly is a recipe for death for many

In Florida, butterfly milkweed is restricted to well-drained sandy soils. Photo by the author.

of our upland plant species, even those that are native to both Florida and areas to the north. A good example is the commonly grown butterfly milkweed (*Asclepias tuberosa*). Butterfly milkweed occurs throughout the eastern half of the country and is a staple of the butterfly garden everywhere. In the prairie states, it is most successful in rich organic soils. In Georgia, it thrives in the red clay hills. In Florida, it will die within weeks if it is not put into a sandy soil with good drainage. If you augment your soil, trying to give a butterfly milkweed what it needed elsewhere, you are very likely to kill it here. This is especially true during the heat of summer when you start to compound your problems with soil-borne fungi and nematodes.

Our typical sandy soils can be very different from each other in terms of drainage, salts, and pH. All these variables may have profound influences on your gardening strategy, so they must be considered up front.

Drainage is influenced by a great number of things. One of these is the size of the sand grain itself. Coarse sands are often found on beach dunes and on historic dunes, such as the Lake Wales Ridge in central Florida. Water percolates rapidly into these sands and is available to plants where their roots are, even if the soil surface appears dry. The other factor affecting drainage is the amount of organic material mixed with the sands. Organic material fills the spaces between sand grains in most yards and in many natural communities. While organics provide some fertility required by plants, they also tend to make it difficult to wet a dry soil surface as water runs off and does not soak in easily until the organics get wet. Organics also slow the percolation of water into the soil column and hold water for longer periods. If your soil is extremely dry during a drought, organic matter will make it difficult to get water down to the roots of your plants. Once it is moist, however, it will hold that water for longer periods of time.

Drainage is also a factor in subsurface conditions; in fact, it is often vastly more significant than anything else. Although many Florida plant

In many parts of Florida, soils are low in organic material and very sandy. Despite that, these soils support a great variety of plant life. Photo by the author.

communities are sandy on the surface, a number are characterized by a clay layer several feet below. In extreme south Florida, an unbroken layer of limestone may be present directly below the soil layer. This "confining" layer prevents water from percolating too deeply and affects rooting depth of many plants because it essentially prevents them from extending through it. In the summer rainy season, these habitats become saturated, and water might stand on the surface for weeks. During the winter dry season, they tend to dry out more quickly than areas of deep sand. Plants of these communities must be adapted to droughty conditions during the winter and spring, and saturated conditions during the summer and early fall. If you notice your yard draining very poorly during the rainy season and/or drying out far too quickly during periods of drought, you need to consider these conditions in your planting decisions.

Soil salinity is a consideration if you live near the coast. Your plants will not only have to be adapted to salts deposited on their foliage by the wind, they must also be tolerant of varying degrees of salts in the soil. Salts can sometimes be carried a good distance inland following a large storm event on the coast, so don't be lulled into thinking that it is not a consideration simply because your yard has been built up and elevated above natural grade. If you are near the coast, you would do best to avoid plants not adapted to salts.

Finally, our sandy soils are often acidic, but in vast geographic regions they are strongly alkaline. If you live in an area where limestone is visible on the surface, you likely have strongly alkaline soils. If you are attempting to landscape areas immediately adjacent to a concrete foundation or driveway, you have the same conditions. Concrete leaches its alkalinity into adjacent soils and can have a large impact on your landscaping efforts. In addition, if your soil contains large amounts of shell, it too is likely alkaline.

Areas of former pineland often have acidic soils, unless they have developed on top of limestone. Some plants, like blueberries, can survive only in strongly acidic soils. Others will decline if the soil is not alkaline enough. The pH of soil affects the ability of plants to absorb nutrients and minerals and it affects the availability of some elements, such as iron. You cannot effectively change the pH of your property, so it is important to select a plant palette adapted to what you have.

Not all soils in Florida are either sandy or acidic. This region near the Aucilla River is one of many where limestone is at or near the surface and the soils are alkaline. Photo by the author.

It is not uncommon that parts of a yard are different from the rest of it. This is especially common if fill has been used to raise the elevation or create a house pad. If you are not sure of your soil's pH, you should either get it tested (most Cooperative Extension offices throughout the state will help with this) or purchase a test kit and do it yourself. Follow the instructions and take soil samples from several inches below the surface. Test widely scattered locations throughout your yard and try to determine the extent of any areas that might be problematic or very different from the rest.

I have used a great deal of ink describing sandy soils, but not all parts of Florida are sandy. Formerly forested systems may have much richer organic soils, while other parts of Florida are underlain by soils high in clays. Regardless, it is important to understand what you have to work with and then develop a plant palette that will thrive in it. For every type of soil, a set of native plants is adapted to it. If you choose wisely, your landscape will develop to its full potential and you will not be faced with replacing plants on a regular basis.

2

Plants and Food

Landscapes must provide food for the wildlife that live there. We accomplish this by careful plant selection and by landscape design. Plants produce food both directly (e.g., fruit, seeds, nuts, leaves) and indirectly (e.g., insects, other wildlife). To design effective landscapes, we need to consider the types of food each plant produces and the best way to put the plants together to maximize their value. We have already done some research to determine the food our target wildlife eat. In this section, I will discuss the roles plants play in food production.

We consider the role of plants in our landscape far too infrequently. Whether a professional designs our landscape or we do it ourselves, landscape architecture is wildlife architecture. Our choice of plants and the way we combine them are the most significant factors in determining the types of wildlife near us. It is time we made that connection and gave it more consideration.

One of the most important roles of plants is that of producing food. As we look at plants for their aesthetic qualities, we rarely also think about what they will produce and what will eat that. Each plant plays some sort of role, even if simply taking up space and preventing another from occupying that spot. By giving this more consideration, we can select plants for our yard that provide the aesthetics we seek as well as the habitat value we desire.

As I've discussed previously, not all wildlife are interested in the seeds, fruit, nuts, and foliage produced by the plants in our landscape. Hawks and owls, for example, are much more interested in lizards and small birds. Friends of mine have watched a pair of Cooper's hawks raise several generations of offspring on the collared doves that also make a home in their

Oaks are one example of a mast-producing woody plant. Nuts and acorns are often difficult for smaller birds to eat, but are excellent food for mammals. Photo by the author.

yard. In a sense, they are raising Cooper's hawk food by actively encouraging the production of collared doves. Regardless of your target wildlife, you need to develop the base of the food pyramid first. That comes with your selection of plants and from consideration of the types of food they produce.

Just as all plants are not created equal, not all fruit, seeds, and nuts have equivalent wildlife value. A fruit is a fruit is a fruit is not true. In laying out your landscape plan, it is important to think more broadly to understand the roles your plants will play in food production and the players that will best fit your team.

To begin, you need to know the types of food each species produces and whether that is important to your overall plan. An easy way to visualize this evaluation is to look at familiar plants: oaks and hollies (*Ilex* spp.). I suspect that all of us know that oaks produce acorns. Many of us in Florida have at least one oak in our yard and are familiar with the acorns that drop each fall. What eats these acorns? Most songbirds are far too small to swallow an acorn, and most of us are not providing for wild turkeys. That leaves mostly wildlife with teeth: squirrels, raccoons, and white-tailed deer. Hollies produce soft round fruit much less attractive to acorn-eating mammals but more universally appealing to songbirds such as cardinals, mockingbirds, and the like. Oaks and hollies are both important wildlife food plants, but they feed very different types of wildlife.

Some plants require wildlife to consume their fruit and seeds so they can successfully disperse and sprout. Fruit that are brightly colored (red, for example) draw the attention of fruit-eating wildlife. This is no accident, but a mutually beneficial relationship that has evolved. Fruit that are hard to see have evolved to avoid detection by wildlife because they often are the type that are chewed up and killed in the process. Others work hard at being totally unattractive, either by covering their seeds with structures such as spines or by concentrating toxic compounds that make them poisonous. Obviously, these latter species have minimal value for a wildlife landscape.

Seasonality

One of the most important food considerations is seasonality. What time of year is the food produced? As we plan our landscape for wildlife habitat, it becomes especially important to have food available year-round. We want to avoid designing a landscape where all the plants produce fruit at the same time of year. We want to stagger it so something is always ready. Fall is the traditional harvest time, for good reason: a wealth of food is usually available. This is true for many of our native plants as well. The leanest time is winter through early spring. If you plan carefully and have plants providing fruit, seeds, and nuts during these months, the value of your landscape to species that depend on these foods will increase dramatically.

Most native elms produce abundant crops of small seeds during the early spring, when little else is available. Photo by the author.

Take the example of elms (*Ulmus* spp.). Elms are wonderful nesting trees for a wide variety of songbirds, but you might not consider them an important food producer. Their seeds are small and surrounded by a papery sheath. They do not look either succulent or tasty, and it's hard to imagine a flock of anything swarming the branches of an elm to get at them. Elms seem unlikely as the poster child for songbird food plants; however, certain elms are particularly important for that purpose. Elms that produce seeds in early spring are among the very few species with this type of food available at this time of year. In the early spring, most plants are leafing out and flowering. Foliage and flowers for insects are abundant, but ripe seeds and fruit are not. Winged and Florida elms (*Ulmus alata* and *U. americana*, respectively) are often alive with activity of seed-eating songbirds when their seeds are ripe in late spring. In contrast, the non-native and widely used drake elm (*Ulmus parvifolia*) produces its seeds in the fall. Watch a drake elm at this time of year and see if anything is in its branches feeding on the seeds. With so many more succulent foods in season, why would anything flock to a drake elm? The truth is, they don't.

The time of year when a plant's food is available to wildlife can also be influenced by the way the ripening process occurs. In some plants, flowering occurs in one discrete season and all the fruit ripens at the same time. Many species seem to have adopted this strategy; in others, flowering and fruiting might occur in several discrete periods, producing batches of fruit several times during the year. A good example of this in Florida is the elderberry (*Sambucus nigra* var. *canadensis*), with flowers and ripe fruit most months of the year. While birds are eating one crop, insects are pollinating the next.

Elderberries in Florida produce flowers and fruit during most months that are excellent food for wildlife. Photo by the author.

Some plants, like this swamp dogwood, produce clusters of fruit that ripen over several weeks—prolonging their value to fruit-eating wildlife. Photo by the author.

In other plants, flowering and fruiting might occur steadily over a protracted period. Plants such as firebush (*Hamelia patens*), depending on latitude, can be in flower nearly every month of the year and produce at least some fruit all the while. Others, like the swamp dogwood (*Cornus foemina*), might bloom in one discrete time period but have fruit that ripens over a period of many weeks. With these strategies, plants increase their harvest season and extend the time for wildlife to consume their offerings. Otherwise, much of this largesse might be wasted and fall to the ground.

Size

Ignore what you may have heard elsewhere; size matters. If you have teeth, the size of a food item may not be relevant. Mammals can grasp food items with their paws and tear or gnaw off chunks with their teeth. Squirrels, for example, couldn't care less how large an acorn is; in fact, they may actually prefer the larger acorns to the smaller ones. For birds, however, size is crucial. Without teeth, they usually end up swallowing their food whole. If the food item is too large to be swallowed, it is too large to eat. If fruit- and seed-eating songbirds are important to you, pay attention to the size of the nuts, seeds, and fruit that each plant produces and select plants appropriately. This seems obvious, but it also seems to be often forgotten.

Different species within the same genus of plants (e.g., oaks and hollies, to name two) produce the same type of food, but it may differ significantly in size. The acorns of a live oak are significantly larger than those of a myrtle oak (*Quercus myrtifolia*); fruits of an American holly (*Ilex opaca*) are larger than those of a yaupon (*Ilex vomitoria*). Species with smaller fruit provide food for many more kinds of songbirds than those with large ones.

Hawthorns (*Crataegus* spp.) provide an especially good example of this. While all hawthorns produce crabapple-type fruit known as "haws" or "hips" (as in rose hips), fruits of the different native species vary widely in size. The summer or yellow haw (currently sold most often as *Crataegus flava*), which occurs throughout the northern two-thirds of Florida, has fruit in the summer months as long as ¾ inch. While larger birds seem to relish it, it is unavailable to small birds. At the other extreme, the littlehip

Hawthorns, such as this littlehip haw, produce small fruit that are easily eaten by even the smallest songbirds. Photo by the author.

Other hawthorns, such as this summer haw, produce larger fruit that are less universally consumed. Photo by the author.

hawthorn (*Crataegus spathulata*) produces tiny fruit, less than ¼ inch long. These can be eaten by even the smallest fruit-eating bird.

Abundance

The sheer quantity of food a plant produces needs to be considered as you plan your landscape. If you have limited space with which to work, it makes no sense to tie up more space than necessary with species known to produce large amounts. Plant a few of these and use the rest of the space for different species that provide different foods. If you have so much of something that it cannot get consumed before it falls to the ground and decomposes or sprouts, you are wasting opportunity.

A good example is beautyberry (*Callicarpa americana*). Beautyberry is a deciduous shrub that occurs statewide, is very adaptable to growing conditions, and is widely available in the nursery trade. Its most attractive trait is the large crops of magenta fruit (white- and lavender-fruited forms are also available), produced in the fall. A beautyberry in fruit can be a beautiful sight—especially to a mockingbird or cardinal looking for an easy meal. Planting one beautyberry in a traditional-sized lot would be sufficient to feed these birds in most cases. Planting a hedge of beautyberry would be a colossal waste of space. This is a good species to use in a mixed hedge.

Some plants, like this American beautyberry, produce so much fruit per plant that only a very few are needed in the landscape. Photo by the author.

Taste

Taste is a difficult concept to quantify for wildlife, but it seems to come into play just as it might for us humans. Foods that seemingly taste the best are also the ones eaten first. Put a plate of Brussels sprouts and jelly beans in front of most children and it's likely a clear choice what they will first consume. It has nothing to do with nutrition, of course. If it did, all of us would be diving into the sprouts. Watch a landscape full of ripe fruit and you might witness something similar. Some fruit seem to disappear as soon as they ripen, and some hang on the plant for months, virtually untouched. I call this the taste factor, although I have no way of evaluating how anything might taste to birds and other wildlife.

Blueberries (*Vaccinium* spp.), blackberries (*Rubus* spp.), and other fruit that taste good to us must rate high on the list for most wildlife too. If you've ever tried to grow these fruits for your own consumption, you know what I mean. When my sons were much younger, they once resorted to eating blueberries while they were green to beat the birds and get some for themselves. They didn't taste as good as the purple ones, but at least they got some.

Other fruit is seemingly on the bottom rung of the taste ladder. I have observed cherry laurels (*Prunus caroliniensis*) and many hollies in full fruit wait patiently for months for something to stop by and consume their crop. To the casual observer, fruit such as these may seem vastly inferior to those consumed first, but these "ugly ducklings" still have fruit in the leanest times of winter, when fruit becomes most significant. Flocks of cedar waxwings and American robins swarm over them in the winter, fueling up for their long migration north. A few plants in the landscape that hold their fruit well into winter can be very important.

Dependability

Not every plant can be counted on to produce a dependable fruit crop each year. For some, it may be two or three years between good crops of nuts, seeds, or fruit. Such plants generally occur in tough habitats, and they require some sort of trigger, such as a fire or an especially good growing season, to produce a full food crop. The sand pine (*Pinus clausa*) produces

Some plants, like this cherry laurel, hold their fruit deep into winter and are thus available to wildlife long after most others have disappeared. Photo by the author.

cones as it matures, but these often do not open and release their seed until the trees are burned. Other species require less extreme conditions. Turkey and bluejack oaks, for example, rarely produce noticeable crops of acorns more frequently than every three or four years. If your landscape plan is designed around wildlife that require these acorns, you will need to add other species to fill in during the lean years.

Sensitivity to cold and drought can also affect the dependability of the plants in your landscape. If your region is prone to late-spring frosts, these can hit at a time when many plants are flowering and setting fruit. Some species will flower again when this happens; others won't. During the years I lived in Kentucky, my backyard peach tree bloomed every spring, and I would watch it in anticipation of the fruit I would get later that

Sand pines often do not release their seed until after a fire. Photo by the author.

summer. Each year, however, a late cold front would freeze the immature fruit and they would drop to the ground. I never harvested a peach. It was just a bad choice for my latitude. Droughts can do the same thing. If you are pushing a water-loving species into a landscape that is not normally moist, the plants may routinely wilt during the dry times and lose their crop. That is why it is important to design your landscape around your growing conditions. If you wish to add species not well adapted to your site, make sure the foundation of your design is sound and will continue to thrive. It's fine to experiment a bit; just don't rely on your experiments. This is especially true for the trees you select. If you plant something intended to dominate a portion of your landscape and have to wait years for it to mature and provide the food and cover you planned, it will create a huge hole in those plans if it perishes because it was not adapted to your conditions.

Sex

Very few consider the sex of the plants incorporated into landscapes. If all we are interested in is form and color, such considerations are probably not important. When we are designing for wildlife, however, it is critical to our success. Many plants are monoecious (meaning: one house); they have either flowers of both sexes or flowers with both male and female parts. Monoecious plants usually pollinate themselves and produce the seeds, nuts, or fruit that wildlife eat. Oaks and hickories, for example, will do just fine by themselves.

Other species are dioecious (two houses). Dioecious plants are either male or female. The male plants will never produce fruit, but you need at least one nearby to pollinate the females. Familiar examples of dioecious plants are the hollies. Only female hollies produce the familiar red berries, but you will get few or none of them without a male nearby. Other common dioecious plants are wax myrtle (*Myrica cerifera*), southern red cedar (*Juniperus virginiana*), and Florida privet (*Forestiera segregata*).

When using dioecious plants in your landscape, plant them in groups, make sure you have a male, and maximize the number of females to maximize fruit production. If you can, try to sex these plants before you purchase them. If the plant has fruit, it is a female. If it doesn't, it could be either. The most reliable method is to take a close look at the flowers. Because most plants flower in the spring, spring is a good time to purchase dioecious plants. Sexing a plant by looking at the flowers is not that difficult, even for small-flowered species. The male flowers release their pollen from the anthers. If you've ever looked at a large flower, like a lily, you know what an anther looks like and you've probably gotten the bright yellow pollen on your clothes or your nose. The female flowers have a receptacle to which the pollen sticks (stigma) and a round base (ovary) where the future seeds (ovules) await the pollination process. It is not difficult to distinguish the pollen-producing flowers from the others, and it is worth the effort. A friend who is an avid birder designed her landscape to maximize its value for songbirds. As part of her plan, she wanted a large hedge of wax myrtle for the fruit and cover it would provide. Ultimately, this hedge materialized from seventeen individual plants. The next year, while waiting for fruit, she discovered that thirteen were males. Only four produced fruit. Though she got the cover value she was looking for, the hedge fell far short of the potential food production her birds needed. If it is not possible to sex your dioecious plants before you install them (many trees, for example, will not flower until they are more than ten years old),

The male and female parts of this pine lily flower are easily seen. Pollen is produced from the anthers (the male part of the flower) and sticks to the stigma atop the ovary (the female part). Photo by the author.

try to plant several in your landscape, and don't be afraid to replace the extra males if you end up with too many.

Foliage

You may wish to plan for certain types of wildlife that feed directly on foliage. Butterfly gardeners routinely take this approach by incorporating the larval food plants of their favorite butterflies into their gardens. Butterfly gardeners quickly appreciate that they will get far more butterflies with plants that caterpillars eat than with flowers to provide nectar for adults. Using plants to be consumed is not confined to butterfly gardens, however. If you live in the northern half of the state, you may want to provide larval food for the magically beautiful luna moth. Its caterpillars feed on the leaves of hickory and sweetgum (*Liquidambar styraciflua*) trees. Another wonderful large silk moth, the polyphemus, occurs nearly statewide and feeds on a variety of oaks.

Many Florida insects make good neighbors. The beautiful luna moth is just one example of an insect that can be easily supported by planting the right plant. Photo by the author.

If you are providing for white-tailed deer, rabbits, or other herbivorous mammals, you will want to select the plant species they prefer. While deer consume acorns and other mast during late summer and fall, they prefer the new growth of many woody species at other times. They especially love plants in the rose family, including hawthorn, apple (*Malus* spp.), and rose (*Rosa* spp.). Deer do not eat grasses, but rabbits will. Deer and rabbits also consume a great many herbaceous wildflowers and the new growth of low-growing woody shrubs, such as blackberry. If these animals are important to you, plan your landscape to include the types of foliage they prefer. If you are trying to discourage them, on the other hand, try to avoid including their favorite plants—what the legal profession might term an "attractive nuisance."

Invertebrates

So far, we have kept our discussion of food to those produced directly by plants. Many songbirds and other wildlife need the types of foods that plants produce indirectly: invertebrates (insects, worms, and other animals without backbones), lizards, and other animal prey. Even songbirds that feed exclusively on fruit and seeds during part of the year often require invertebrates at other times—especially during the summer months, for themselves and their young. Invertebrates form an extremely important foundation of the food web, and they must be present in our landscapes if we are to be successful.

We can do many things to build a healthy and productive invertebrate food base. One is to plant species known to be favorites of butterfly and moth caterpillars. Such an approach requires use of larval food plants specific to our part of Florida. Many caterpillars of butterfly and moth species feed on different plants in different parts of the country. The eastern tiger swallowtail, for example, lays its eggs on certain cherries (*Prunus* spp.) and ashes (*Fraxinus* spp.) in New England and the Upper Midwest, but ignores them in the Deep South. In much of Florida, the preferred larval food of tiger swallowtail is sweetbay (*Magnolia virginiana*). Consult with local butterfly and moth experts and their writings for information relevant to your location in Florida before investing in large shade trees and shrubs for your landscape.

Insects, such as this European honey bee, are critical to the pollination of many plants in the landscape. This bee is pollinating a red maple. Photo by the author.

Also be aware that caterpillars of different butterflies and moths may not be equal in food value, accessibility, or abundance. It's just not that simple. Small songbirds need small larvae for their young nestlings. Large caterpillars will not work.

Some caterpillars are toxic and not eaten at all by birds or mammals. Examples are the caterpillars of milkweed butterflies (monarchs and queens), the oleander moth, and the butterflies that feed on Dutchman's pipe (*Aristolochia* spp.). Many plants evolve defenses to herbivory (eating of foliage) by storing toxic or bad-tasting chemicals in their leaves. The insects adapted to feed on these plants store the chemicals in their body tissues, and the chemicals often then protect them from higher level predators. Lizards and insects may be immune to the toxins stored by these caterpillars, but the great majority of birds and mammals learn to leave them alone, because eating them makes them ill.

Caterpillars are a critical food source for birds such as this hooded warbler. You can provide this food with a well-planned butterfly garden. Photo by Christina Evans, with permission.

But for all the importance of caterpillars to many songbirds, a fixation on them ignores the great value of the many other invertebrate prey that are not caterpillars; namely, other insects, worms, spiders, and the like. Success comes from creating conditions in your yard that promote a healthy ecology where invertebrate life will thrive. In the vast majority of cases, a healthy ecosystem in your yard will produce all the invertebrate food required by wildlife, and more often than not, native plants will provide better conditions than non-native ones.

Invertebrates have gotten a bad rap over the years. We have become brainwashed that "bugs" in the landscape require some sort of response from us. The "see a bug, call us" mentality has created a mindset that these creatures are somehow evil and need to be taken care of. We need to rid ourselves of this concept if we are going to be successful at creating landscapes that provide wildlife habitat.

While some invertebrates can become serious pests, the vast majority are important components of the natural community. We can deal with the serious pests by targeting them specifically: using integrated pest management practices instead of wholesale slaughter. Blanket "pest control" eradicates the entire foundation of the food pyramid in a yard and upsets the delicate balance of nature we are seeking to develop. In almost every case, the serious pests are the first to rebound after chemical treatment, and their predators (the species that might control them naturally) are the last. Over time, this form of pest control is a self-perpetuating problem that actually gets worse and causes it never to be resolved.

Take the issue of aphids, for example. Left unchecked, aphids will multiply and eventually suck the sap and the life out of certain plants. I have had plants with aphids lose nearly all their aboveground foliage. When this starts to happen, I am always tempted to treat the plants with insecticide, but I have learned that if I am patient the ladybugs or lacewings will eventually arrive. These insects and their larvae feed exclusively on aphids. Once they find the aphid infestation, they begin to feed and slowly multiply. Eventually, they eat every aphid and depart. New aphids might

In a native landscape, many insect problems are controlled by other insects. Certain insects such as this ladybug beetle are extremely effective predators of aphids. Photo by the author.

return, but ladybugs and lacewings do also. It is a natural cycle, and it works. If you spray the aphids, you will also kill the ladybugs, lacewings, and their aphid-eating larvae. The aphids will return much more quickly than their predators, and next time, the problem will be worse.

The most important way to manage invertebrates in a landscape is to adopt the practices of integrated pest management. Such an approach directs us to target the real problems and to rely on more natural approaches whenever possible. Often, the problems we see are not really problems at all. Leaves being chewed, for example, are a sign of life in the landscape. The invertebrates doing the feeding are providing food for birds, lizards, and other wildlife. It is very rare that these types of invertebrates multiply to large enough numbers to cause serious injury to plants. If they do, resolve the problem with an insecticide that targets only the problem.

Treat problems only when they are problems, not through routine maintenance designed to ensure a problem never occurs. Use plants that are not as susceptible to these types of problems. Taking the right plant/right place approach to landscaping will solve most of the problems you might have with pests. Finally, let nature take control whenever and wherever possible.

Flowers

Insects can be attracted to your landscape by flowers. If you spend any time in a garden, you quickly learn that not every flower attracts insects and that different flowers seem to attract different kinds. You may also observe that some of the best flowers for certain types of insects hardly fit our normal image of a flower at all. During spring migration, warblers and other insect-eating songbirds often drop out of the sky en masse to feast on the small insects pollinating various spring-blooming shade trees. The flowers of oaks and red mulberry (*Morus rubra*) are especially good magnets, and they are dependable spots for watching these beautiful songbirds in the spring. Some flowers, like those of pines, are designed to be pollinated by wind. These plants are not good choices if one of your main interests is feeding insect-eating songbirds during spring migration. It's the canopy of insect-pollinated trees that come alive during flowering time.

Trees such as this laurel oak produce thousands of tiny flowers in the spring that attract pollinating insects. As the insects arrive, these trees become magnets to migratory songbirds looking to restore their energy supplies. Photo by the author.

The flowers of shrubs and ground covers can also be important. Butterflies and moths are important food sources for many wildlife; bees much less so. Often, a fairly clear difference exists between bee-pollinated flowers and those most often pollinated by butterflies and other insects. Landscapes should have both, but you will feed more wildlife with butterfly garden flowers.

Bark

If you venture into one of Florida's pinelands, you are more likely to see songbirds foraging on the trunks and branches of pines than anywhere else. Most pines develop a shaggy/flaky bark with a wide range of hiding places for insects and other invertebrates; thus, as food for wildlife, pines are far more important for the insects hiding under their bark than for the food produced in their cones. Trees and shrubs vary greatly in bark patterns and in ability to provide invertebrates for wildlife. Smooth-barked

Right: Pines and other rough-barked trees harbor insects and are very important to insect-eating birds and other wildlife. Photo by the author.

Below: Trees with smooth bark, such as this sycamore, provide virtually no cover for insects and are very poor choices for wildlife because of this. Photo by the author.

trees, such as sycamore (*Platanus occidentalis*) and maples, are essentially dead zones in this regard. Trees with crevices and shaggy bark are much better.

Mulches

The other significant part of a landscape for production of invertebrates is the upper surface of the soil, under leaf litter, and within the organic matter that develops just below. For this reason, the best mulches are those that decompose, not those that rest on the surface as decoration. I am constantly amazed at the average homeowner's activity each fall, raking leaves, bagging them, hauling them to the curb for disposal—a huge expenditure of energy to rid themselves of something so valuable. At these

Leaf litter and other organic mulches provide ideal conditions for earthworms and other invertebrates. Photo by the author.

times, my wife and I take the back seats out of our vehicle and rescue this refuse for our own landscape purposes. Leaf litter and other organic mulches are rich in worms and other invertebrates. Such conditions provide exceptional feeding areas for a wide variety of wildlife that depend on this food source. Mulches that resist decomposition, such as cypress, produce very poor conditions for the production of invertebrate food and should be avoided in a landscape for wildlife.

Other Animal Prey

With a strong foundation of plantings, you are also creating the conditions necessary for habitat for other species. Predators and other specialty feeders may not be interested in the food your plants produce or the invertebrates, but they can be supported by the wildlife drawn by those resources. If your landscape is producing anoles and other lizards, you are also feeding the birds and reptiles relying on them. If your landscape is alive with songbirds, a few may fall prey to hawks and other predators. This is not wrong; it is natural.

3

Plants and Cover

Cover is a function of the individual plants you select and the landscape design that brings them together. As discussed in chapter 1, some wildlife species prefer open spaces while others require dense vegetation. Cover requirements vary greatly between species. You must meet the cover requirements for each wildlife species you have targeted.

Cover is a somewhat complex concept. It must include enough space to meet the territorial requirements of each species as well as the proper conditions for their life requirements. When food is abundant, most wildlife require a bit less space than when it's scarce. There is a bottom threshold, a minimum they can tolerate, and that is why most of us lack the space to landscape for a Florida panther or black bear. These species occupy home ranges in excess of 10,000 acres and require extensive natural landscapes to meet their complex food and cover requirements. Most desirable species, however, can fit in the typical lot size, and can live in our neighborhoods if we can extend our reach beyond our own yards as well.

Cover is not static. For most songbirds, nesting cover is different from foraging cover, and winter cover may be very different from the types of cover required during the breeding season. The Carolina wren, for example, will use a nest box for nesting cover, but it needs much more for survival in an area. It needs a dense thicket for hiding and insect-rich areas for foraging. If you hang a wren house from a tree limb in the open, it might never be used by wrens, even if they're in the neighborhood. If you have plenty of insects, but no quiet thicket where they can hide, they may never feed in your landscape. You'll need all the components to provide effectively for this species. The same is true for all species of wildlife.

The native Carolina wren prefers a house near a thicket of good cover. This same house in the open would likely go unused. Photo by the author.

Just as diets might change over the course of the year, cover requirements also often change between breeding and nonbreeding months. In their breeding range, American robins are rather solitary birds. There, they typically nest in the lower branches of dense trees and shrubs and forage on the ground for earthworms and other invertebrates. While in Florida during the winter, however, robins mass in large flocks and forage in fruit-bearing trees such as hollies and cherries. This is the same bird, but with very different behaviors and habitat needs depending on season.

Cover, therefore, is the collection of all the space and structure required by an animal to live, breed, and survive. The space is merely a mathematical equation. The structure is the component you control through your plantings.

Different plants have different attributes that affect the types and quality of cover they provide. As discussed above for food, even plants of the same genus (oaks, for example) have different growth characteristics that influence their roles in providing cover. Each species is unique in the type of foliage it produces and the way that foliage is structured. That is why most of us can easily distinguish one species from another, even at a distance. You don't need a botany degree to distinguish a live oak from a cabbage palm or even from the more closely related laurel oak. If they look different to us, they surely look different to the wildlife that depend on them for their survival. Let us examine some of the most important attributes influencing wildlife cover value.

Size

Size matters for cover. Different wildlife species use different layers of the landscape. Some species prefer life high in the treetops, while others nest only in the shrub layer or spend much of their time near the ground. Therefore, you need tall trees for some wildlife and shorter trees and shrubs for others. Before you select a plant to use in your landscape, you need to know how tall it will grow and how wide it will spread. Most likely, you will need a few tall species and more short ones. Most landscapes need a variety of heights to be effective. Creating layers is important.

Too often, we do not consider how tall plants will be at maturity or how landscapes change over time as the plants mature. We fail to consider that the live oak we plant this year as a 3-gallon sapling will eventually reach 75 feet, with a spread of almost half that distance. In some situations, this may be exactly what you need, but in small yards or tight quarters, you should probably select an oak with a smaller stature or narrower crown. You need to look to the future to visualize your landscape once the plants have matured. A plant often plays a decidedly different role as it grows. A good example is the common southern red cedar. As a small tree, the red cedar is a dense mound of prickly foliage that shields just about everything from view. At this size, it is often used as a privacy hedge. As it matures, this same plant becomes a tall, straight-trunked tree with all the cover in its crown, 60 feet in the air. Your landscape will change as it

Above: Sapling red cedars provide dense shrubby cover. Photo by the author.

Right: A mature red cedar provides cover only in its crown, more than 40 feet above the ground. Photo by the author.

matures, but your plan should consider those changes so you don't lose essential cover as it does.

Foliage Density

The foliage of some plants is dense while that of others is not. Foliage density is the result of a variety of factors, including leaf size and branch structure, but the bottom line is that certain plants are much better than others at hiding wildlife from view. Dense foliage is especially important in creating hiding, nesting, and sleeping cover. When engaging in those activities, it is dangerous to be visible. Most birds build their nests where they are well secluded, not where they can be seen. On the other hand, singing male songbirds will often select a perch in the open so they can advertise their presence. By understanding the inherent foliage density of the plants you select, you can be more effective in creating the kinds of cover you need and putting plants together to make up for individual shortcomings of certain plants that are not especially dense.

Plants vary greatly in the density of their foliage. This pigmy fringetree is not a good choice either for nesting cover or simply for hiding. Photo by the author.

Evergreen vs. Deciduous

It is important to consider whether a plant is evergreen or deciduous. Though both are equally good at providing cover during the summer when most species are nesting, deciduous plants fall short of providing winter cover. That does not mean that deciduous plants are inferior. There is good reason to use a great many of them in the landscape. Even in the winter, they may provide important food and open perches, but without at least some areas of evergreen plants, most wildlife will not have their need for cover completely met and will be forced to leave after leaf-fall. For this reason, wildlife landscape plans should be designed with areas of evergreen winter cover.

Thorniness

Thorny plants are often underappreciated or even avoided by homeowners, but they can play a significant role in the wildlife landscape. For the small songbird or mammal being chased by a predator, the ability to slip into a dense bramble can mean the difference between escape and death. Thorniness is really a relative term. Some plants, like the cockspur haw (*Crataegus crus-galli*) and sweet acacia (*Acacia farnesiana*), come armed with thorns and hooks that make them nearly impenetrable. Others, like the Chickasaw plum (*Prunus angustifolia*) and Walter's viburnum (*Viburnum obovatum*), simply produce a myriad of little side-shoot branches that function essentially as thorns. Thorny plants can be effective if they are located out of regular pathways and planted to anchor areas in out-of-the-way places where you will not be walking or entertaining. These thickets can be surrounded by more user-friendly plants to reduce the risk of impalement. Such effort may seem too great, but the results will be worth it. If you plant a thicket anchored by thorny plants in the center, watch where the songbirds head each time a disturbance surfaces in your landscape.

Thorny plants, like this tough bumelia, provide excellent escape and nesting cover. Photo by the author.

Branch Structure

Although I often have a difficult time conveying exactly what I mean by branch structure, it is certainly obvious that different plants have different branching patterns and branches of different strengths. Some plants provide relatively dense cover, but their branches are too flimsy to support the weight or the nest of most songbirds. Others, like the live oak, may have massive limbs that can certainly support the weight of any animal but lack the smaller forks needed for the nests of small birds. A bald eagle normally seeks a large living pine with a broad flat crown to support its massive nest. A cardinal requires something completely different.

For the most part, nesting birds are best served by trees and shrubs that produce strong branches from the main trunk in a variety of sizes and at different angles. I learned this lesson early in life. When I was a child in Wisconsin, the streets of my neighborhood were lined by American elms (*Ulmus americana*). This was, of course, before Dutch elm disease came into the picture and wiped them out. Each year, these trees served the nesting needs of a great many songbirds (especially those of the northern oriole), and during the winter the empty nests in their branches were

The best nesting trees are those with great diversity in branch sizes and branch forks. Few trees meet this condition better than the native winged elm. Photo by the author.

obvious after leaf-fall. Walking home after school, I could see the diversity of nest types and the different positions within the trees where the nests were placed. Elms are great nesting trees because their branches are strong and occur in a range of sizes that tend to fork at upright angles. Because of this, birds can find a fork that suits their needs, and their nest will be supported throughout the season. Other trees and shrubs have similar characteristics and are equally good, for example, red cedar and plums.

Combining Plants

Cover is not a function solely of individual plants, but also of landscapes. Here, the whole is more than the sum of the parts. While individual plants may not provide all that might be required, you can blend different plants to achieve what you need. Creating a mixed hedge instead of a single-species one is a good example. By themselves, shrubs such as marlberry (*Ardisia escallonioides*) and beautyberry offer very limited value as nesting and hiding cover. Their branches are simply too weak, and their foliage is not dense enough. The value of these plants lies mostly in the food they produce. In a mixed hedge with species such as yaupon holly (*Ilex vomitoria*), Walter's viburnum, and southern wax myrtle, the varied foliage and intermingled branches of the collective creates conditions that maximize the attributes of each.

This effect is especially true for areas dominated by ground covers. In a dense woodland setting, solitary ferns do little to hide foraging or ground-nesting wildlife. In a mass, these same ferns shield the presence of even medium-sized animals. Mixing several ferns together often increases their cover value even more. You can then optimize this area of your landscape by adding low-growing woody species such as coffees (*Psychotria* spp.) and rouge plant (*Rivina humilis*). By themselves, each species has limitations. As a community, individuals function together to provide much more. Birds such as ovenbirds and thrushes require this type of cover to feel comfortable, and so do many other species that use the forest floor.

There are often good reasons to use plants in your landscape that are not especially effective for providing cover. Sometimes, the plants in question are excellent food producers but have weak branches or an open

Rouge plant, planted in mass, provides excellent cover for ground-dwelling wildlife. Photo by the author.

habit. One of my personal favorites, the fringetree (*Chionanthus virginicus*), is a good example of a small tree with little cover value for wildlife, but good value as a food plant. Use these food-producing species against a backdrop of better cover-producing species. If you use a fringetree, for example, place it adjacent to an area of better cover. In this way, wildlife will not have to venture far from cover to eat, and their safety will be protected.

4

Water in the Landscape

This book is devoted primarily to plants and their use in creating habitat for wildlife. Plants provide two essential elements of wildlife habitat: food and cover. The third component, water, is mostly independent of plant palette and landscape design. Despite this, I would be remiss if I didn't include a small section on water. Wildlife get the water they need from a variety of sources. A few species do not drink at all, and many get what they need from the food they consume. Most, however, require free-standing water, and your landscape will become habitat only when you provide it.

Assuming you have no natural stream or pond in your landscape, you can provide water in a variety of ways, from a simple birdbath to a man-made pond or stream. Water features add an element of movement and beauty to the landscape not duplicated by other means and a focal point that enhances your wildlife viewing opportunities. Most wildlife in your landscape will eventually use your water feature. By keeping an eye on it, you might observe many species you never even knew were there.

In our landscape, Alexa and I have provided water in several ways. In key locations, we placed standard birdbaths. While most birdbaths are not especially beautiful or exciting landscape features, they serve the purpose of providing water to those species that can reach and use them, but because the water is several feet off the ground, it is inaccessible to many species that cannot fly or climb; therefore, we also created a pond with a small stream flowing from a second small pool above it.

The pond and its small stream provide an entirely different experience and attract wildlife in a very different way. For one, they allow wildlife, such as frogs and toads, to simply exist. Over the years, our small pond at the end of the stream has provided for pig frogs and leopard frogs—both

Water features are important for wildlife and enhance viewing opportunities. Photo by the author.

species that I never expected to see in the heart of suburbia where we live. The moving shallow water of the stream is especially attractive to migratory songbirds. During most springs, we get as many as 25 different species of warblers as well as buntings, grosbeaks, and thrushes using our stream. In the early morning and late evening, they literally line up for their turn in the stream, bathing and drinking in the shallow cascading water. They do not share the birdbaths with our resident cardinals, blue jays, and fish crows, and without the stream they might not stay with us.

Both types of water features are important to the type of wildlife habitat Alexa and I have worked to create. Many resources are available to help you build a water feature. If doing so interests you, don't be intimidated if you are not typically a "handyperson." There are many designs and styles to choose from, and many are easy to install. Some, such as a preformed pond, simply require you to dig a hole. Others, such as the one we have, require some electrical work for the pump and a bit more installation savvy.

Regardless of how you supply water, some important points should be carefully considered to make your water feature effective for wildlife. Water features are not lawn ornaments, and it is not simply a question of whether to provide water. The question is the way it is provided. Ignoring the considerations below can make an otherwise wonderful water feature useless.

Water Depth

Water depth is critical. If you are providing water for truly aquatic species, such as fish, your water depth must provide sufficient oxygen for them to breathe and sufficient escape cover to survive. Shallow water quickly loses oxygen as temperatures rise. During the summer months, shallow water in the sun may become too depleted of oxygen to support even small minnows and other aquatic life. In addition, predators quickly learn to hunt the shallows. If a pond has no deepwater areas into which to flee, most aquatic wildlife will be eliminated in a short period of time.

For other species, such as songbirds, the depth of the water determines the size of animal using it. If you carefully watch songbirds at a water feature, you will notice that each seeks out a depth at which it is comfortable. Large birds, such as crows, bathe in or drink from water many inches deep. Small birds, such as Carolina wrens, will do so only in water of a few inches at most. Long-legged wading birds forage for fish in deeper water than short-legged species. Most wildlife choose a spot in a water feature based on water depth and their body size.

You can use these criteria to your advantage. If there are species you wish to exclude, design your water feature to a depth that is either too deep or shallow for them. If you wish to include wildlife of all sizes, design a water feature with gently sloping sides to an ultimate depth that allows even large species to be comfortable. Gently sloping sides are inclusive; steep sides eliminate many species that might otherwise use it. This is true whether you are considering a birdbath or designing a pond.

Birds select the water depth with which they are most comfortable. This female Northern cardinal is enjoying its turn in a well-designed birdbath. Photo by Christina Evans, with permission.

You can rectify the problem of a steep-sided water feature by placing well-anchored stones or other structures on the bottom of the feature under the water. Smaller birds can sometimes be coaxed into using deeper water with a landing area giving access to a water depth they prefer. Designing a shallow-water lip or shelf in a deep-water pond can work in much the same way. If you have a water feature already in place, it would be worthwhile trying to retrofit it in this manner to make it more wildlife friendly. If you are starting from scratch, do things correctly from the start and select a birdbath or design a pond with gently sloping sides.

Surface of Water Feature

Some birdbaths come with a shiny, slick enamel glaze. While beautiful as pottery pieces, they are potentially life threatening to songbirds. Just as you would not purposely remove the mat from your shower or tub before running the water, you should not expect songbirds and other wildlife to be comfortable or safe in a water feature with a slick bottom. Wildlife need a rough surface for the traction it provides. As they venture down into the water for a drink or bath, they are aware of the slick nature of the substrate. Should they need traction to push off and escape a predator, a slippery surface can doom them. When you plan your water feature, remember that you are not selecting for beauty, but functionality. Choose wisely.

Location of Water Feature

The final major consideration for your water feature is where to place it, not necessarily the exact location in your landscape, but the context of

Birdbaths should be located near cover, but not directly in dense cover. Photo by the author.

its location. Water is necessary to wildlife, but accessing it is dangerous. If you've ever watched a wildlife documentary on television, you've witnessed how dangerous it is to access water. Wildlife congregate around the watering hole. The camerapersons know this and so do the predators. Wildlife approach water cautiously because the individuals still alive have learned it too. Therefore, water features should never be placed in the open or where they are surrounded by dense cover. Their placement needs to be a compromise between the two.

Baths and ponds located in an open location may never get used. Any potential prey animal, such as a songbird, is put in extreme jeopardy if it ventures into a water feature in an open landscape. Getting a drink, for example, requires the animal to lower its head and take its eyes off the world around it. Predators wait for this moment; they take advantage of it and make their move. A small bird, sitting in a birdbath and taking a drink, is a screaming advertisement to the rest of the world that it is available and willing to be eaten. Few escape if they ignore this danger, and far fewer return to risk another chance.

For most of the same reasons, dense cover near a water feature is equally dangerous, maybe even more so. If you think back to the wildlife documentary example above, where do the lions lie in wait? They are not roaming across the vast expanses of open grassland hoping to encounter something. They are patiently waiting, hidden in the tall grass, next to the watering hole. Why waste energy wandering when you can relax and wait, knowing that eventually the prey will come to you? Predators, from neighborhood cats to hawks and crows, are ever present even in residential landscapes. Small songbirds, mice, and other wildlife are unlikely to use your water feature if the vegetation around it is too dense.

Place your water feature near escape cover, but not within it. If you have some dense shrubs or ground cover several feet away, wildlife can remain relatively hidden as they approach the water, and they can survey the situation before they make their final move to it. Then, if there is a disturbance or a predator, they have a short distance to retreat and escape. Of course, all this is moot if your water feature is meant to be a feeder for hawks . . .

5

Plant Selection

I have devoted a lot of discussion to other topics before getting to this part of the book. I hope I've given you a clearer understanding of what wildlife landscaping is all about and why you should embark on this new landscape approach. You have a better concept of the meaning of wildlife habitat and the changes that might be necessary in your existing landscape to make it better as habitat. You understand you must design your landscape around the wildlife you want to attract and that your landscape plan and choice of plants must take your existing growing conditions into consideration. You also now realize that each plant species has its own food and cover characteristics and that you must select those that best provide for your long-term goals. Each of us has different goals and landscape settings, so there is no one plant (or landscape plan) that is best. Given that, it is time to look at some of the best native plants for Florida wildlife landscaping.

The native plants highlighted in this book have characteristics that make them especially good providers of both food *and* cover for wildlife; therefore, species such as the river birch (*Betula nigra*) that provide almost nothing for wildlife in terms of food but have value for nesting have been omitted. I have avoided including species of value to only a limited group of wildlife; instead, I have focused on those with more universal or widespread value. I have also not included plants that are either so uncommon or difficult to grow as to be impractical for most landscape situations.

This does not mean that every plant described here will be easy to find in your local nursery or even widely available from nurseries that specialize in native plants. It is my belief that you should not be deterred from selecting plants you want simply because they might take some time to locate. Your landscape and the goals you have established for it are worth the effort. For that reason, I have included some plants that are uncommon in the nursery trade if they have good wildlife value as well as good landscaping potential. It is my hope that their inclusion here will encourage their more widespread availability in the future. Market forces are especially responsive to demand. If a market is created, smart businesses will supply it.

My plant list does not include the vast assortment of herbaceous plants (grasses and wildflowers) that have value in a native plant landscape. While many species of wildlife feed extensively on their foliage and seeds, and the habitat they create in the understory can be especially significant, it is not possible to include them all within the scope of this work. I am leaving that discussion for a future book. Realize that your landscape plan might require you to use some of the wonderful ferns, grasses, and wildflowers native to Florida. The plants discussed in this book are limited to woody species, that is, trees and shrubs.

This list is not exhaustive, nor is it intended to be. The information is presented with the intention of guiding you in assessing the best choices for your landscape. Over time and with experience, you may wish to add additional species that have attributes important to you. Never rely solely on someone else's list for all your choices. Do not be afraid to experiment, to try something that makes sense, or to change your mind based on acquired experience. That is what good land managers learn to do, and that is your new role.

In the text above, I have discussed the various attributes you should consider when evaluating the wildlife value of particular plants. In the discussion that follows, I have attempted to assemble the relevant information you will need for that evaluation. Descriptions of aesthetic considerations and growing condition requirements are also included; this is, after all, a book for gardeners.

For simplicity, I have lumped all the plants into two categories: monoecious and dioecious. While this division is not strictly accurate from a plant taxonomy standpoint, it makes the discussion easier for the average reader. For the purposes of this book, monoecious plants are capable of producing fruit by themselves, and dioecious plants need a separate male plant to pollinate female plants. If I have labeled a plant "dioecious," you will need more than one to produce fruit, and only the females will bear it.

Just as most of us use a binomial naming system for ourselves that includes a name we use with friends and a second name that identifies our family (John Smith, for example), a similar naming approach is standard for plants and animals, only in Latin. All maples have the same genus name: *Acer*—the first of their two Latin names and the part roughly equivalent to "Smith" in the John Smith example above. This name distinguishes the maples from the oaks and hickories, for example—plants not closely related to them. The second half of the Latin name identifies each species from the others in the same way that "John Smith" is different from his close relative "Jane Smith." A red maple (*Acer rubrum*) is unique from a sugar maple (*Acer saccharum* subsp. *floridanum*), but it is obvious that both are related since they share the same genus name. My brothers and I share the same last name, but we have unique first names. It is no more complicated than that.

I have arranged the plants in this book alphabetically by the common names of their genus to help you find them more easily. The maples are listed under "Maples" (not under *Acer*) and then listed alphabetically by their Latin species names. Therefore, the red maple (*Acer rubrum*) precedes the Florida sugar maple (*Acer saccharum* subsp. *floridanum*). At times, I have separated families when their common names are widely known and used. Therefore, the elms and the hackberries are under separate headings even though both are in the elm family, and black walnut is not included with the rest of the hickories though it too is a "hickory."

Although this approach is meant to make it easier for readers, there is no substitute for learning the Latin. Latin names are universally used in all nations and are unique to each plant and animal. Many common names are not commonly used, and none are unique to one species. An author referring to a "hog plum" might be writing about a thorny shrub with large yellow fruit (*Ximenia americana*) or a medium-sized tree in the plum family (*Prunus umbellata*). You may not wish to learn the Latin names provided here, but pay attention to them to ensure the plant you are actually looking for is the plant you want and not something completely different.

This "hog plum," *Ximenia americana*, is a very different plant from the spring-blooming *Prunus umbellata* shown on page 141. Common names can be confusing, so don't ignore the Latin ones. Photo by the author.

The index at the back is designed to assist you in locating individual species so they can be more easily found in the text. Each plant is listed in the index by common and Latin names. For species with multiple common names, I have tried to list all the most commonly used ones. Wildlife names are listed only by common name as I have chosen not to use Latin names for them in the text.

Extreme south Florida has a flora unique to itself. Many of these plants can be used farther north, in locations where winter temperatures dependably stay no colder than the upper 20s Fahrenheit. I have had experience growing many south Florida plants in Pinellas County. For others, I have had to rely on published accounts and discussions with experts. I have included a few others that I have not grown extensively and have noted those that may be adapted only to extreme south Florida. None of these species should be attempted in colder regions of the state.

Similarly, many native plants restricted to extreme north Florida can be successfully grown in the more central regions of the state, given the right soil, light, and moisture conditions. I mention those with which I have the most experience in Pinellas County. Some, however, will not produce fruit, nuts, or seeds without sufficient days of cold weather. I have not included those most difficult to grow and have made note of others that are not well adapted to locations that don't reliably go below freezing in the winter.

I have included a small section of additional resources at the end of the book to direct you to other books, organizations, Web sites, and the like that might assist you in developing your wildlife landscape. No single work can include everything you need to know, and reference lists eventually grow out of date. Start with this book, explore other resources and the ideas of others, stay in tune with the new ideas and information of the future, and always learn by observing and being willing to experiment.

Much of our knowledge of wildlife gardening is in its infancy. Wildlife biologists have a difficult time assessing the relative importance of individual native plants for each wildlife species in a natural setting. The value of each plant becomes even more obscured when we place it in areas disturbed by urbanization. Very few studies have been done of wildlife in urban landscapes, and far fewer have looked at the relative importance of different plants and landscape styles. In a way, then, we are on the cutting edge of a new wildlife management paradigm, directed at vast expanses of heretofore neglected regions of potential habitat. What we are attempting is not an exact science. Our primary tools will be the plants we install and nurture in our home landscapes and our willingness to observe.

PLANT DESCRIPTIONS

Acacias

The legumes are among the largest families of flowering plants in the world and include some of the world's most important food crops (beans and peas), forage crops (clover and alfalfa), and favorite ornamentals. All produce hard, nutritious, beanlike or pealike seeds enclosed in a tough, leathery pod. Most have nitrogen-fixing bacteria associated with their root systems, which serve to enrich the soil and improve the forage quality of foliage. As such, they are frequently fed on by a wide variety of browsing animals as well as the caterpillars of butterflies and moths, and a great many other insects. Many legumes have showy blooms pollinated by bees. Four genera of native woody legumes—the acacias, locusts, tamarinds, and blackbeads—have wildlife value. Of these, only the acacias are commonly available from commercial nurseries and are discussed below. Acacias are monoecious, highly salt tolerant, and very adaptable to growing conditions. Several species are very rare in Florida. Only the sweet acacia is widely available for landscaping purposes. Its close relative, pineland acacia, is essentially a dwarf version and valuable mostly for creating impenetrable thickets.

Sweet Acacia (*Acacia farnesiana*)

Sweet acacia is the most widely distributed native acacia in Florida and can be grown statewide in sunny, well-drained coastal and interior soils. Its small, feathery leaves are deciduous for a brief period in winter, and the extremely fragrant flowers are most abundant in early spring as the new leaves develop. Flowers and the beanlike seed pods may be produced in nearly every month. Each pod contains about six rounded, ¼-inch seeds that have only marginal food value to most wildlife. Sweet acacia is extremely thorny, with spines on the trunk and branches and at the

Sweet acacia (*Acacia farnesiana*). Photo by the author.

leaf nodes. Thorns greatly enhance its cover value for nesting birds and other wildlife but make it necessary to plant the tree away from walkways and recreation areas. Use sweet acacia as an anchor for a wildlife thicket and in a location where the scent of its flowers can be fully appreciated. Sweet acacia is susceptible to thorn bugs. Although these insects are fascinating to look at, they will decimate your tree if allowed to reproduce unchecked.

Pineland Acacia (*A. pinetorum*)

Pineland acacia is a shrub or very small tree of central and south Florida that rarely exceeds 6 feet in height and normally grows in open pinelands and the edges of hammock woodlands. It is nearly identical in appearance to the sweet acacia, differing mostly in overall size and the size of its leaflets, which are about half the length of those of the sweet acacia. Because of its smaller stature, pineland acacia has little cover value for wildlife

Pineland acacia (*Acacia pinetorum*). Photo by the author.

except when planted in a mass to form a low thorny thicket. This plant is best used in open, sunny locations and thrives in alkaline soils.

American Beech

American beech (*Fagus grandifolia*) is a major component of the eastern deciduous forest in North America, but its natural range in Florida is confined mostly to the Panhandle and a few scattered hammocks in the northern peninsula. It is not adaptable to Florida landscapes much beyond its natural range. This is a large, long-lived deciduous tree that may reach 100 feet at maturity, but its growth rate is relatively slow. It can also reproduce by root suckers and produces small groves if allowed to do so. Because beech is adapted to reproducing in the dense shade of the temperate mixed forest, young beeches do best when planted in partial shade. Saplings will eventually become dominant shade trees. American beech grows best in moist, fertile soils. Its large crown and branches provide cover for many woodland wildlife species, and its branching structure is ideal for many nesting birds. American beech is monoecious. The ¾-inch, triangular beechnuts are a relished food source in the fall for many mammals and some songbirds, including jays and chickadees. They also are edible for human consumption. Good nut crops are not produced annually, but occur every two or three years. The American beech also serves as a larval food source for a number of moths, making it useful for songbirds that feed on caterpillars. Its smooth bark, however, does not provide good hiding places for insects or foraging habitat for wildlife that might consume them. If you have the space and the growing conditions for this species, American beech is a beautiful and grand shade tree and valuable as an anchor in a large mixed deciduous hardwood forest planting. This species is not salt tolerant.

American beech (*Fagus grandifolia*). Photo by the author.

Ashes

Ashes (*Fraxinus* spp.) are medium to large deciduous trees placed in the olive family. Their compound leaves are similar in appearance to those of hickories, but they are opposite each other in pairs on the branches. In the fall, their leaves generally turn a bright yellow. Ashes eventually produce large, rounded canopies that provide excellent cover for wildlife. They are fast growing and may add as much as six feet of new growth per year when young. They are dioecious. The 1–2½-inch flattened winged seeds ripen in late summer or early fall. Birds such as cardinals sometimes feed on them, but they are used mostly by squirrels and other rodents. Ashes are hosts to the eastern tiger swallowtail butterfly in north Florida, a wide variety of moth caterpillars statewide, and other insects. Such invertebrates benefit songbirds. All our ashes are moderately tolerant of salt and very adaptable to a range of growing conditions. They perform best when grown in

White ash (*Fraxinus americana*). Shirley Denton, with permission.

sunny locations. Stressed trees are susceptible to a variety of viral, bacterial, and fungal problems that rarely are lethal, but cause leaf loss and/or stunting. Three species of ashes occur in Florida.

White Ash (*Fraxinus americana*)

White ash is a large tree (often to 60 feet) resident to fertile woodland soils in north and north central Florida. It is adaptable and can be used into central Florida without problems. Of the three native ashes in Florida, this is the most adapted to upland locations. White ash gets its common name from its leaves, which have a distinctive whitish bloom on the underside. Each leaf is usually composed of seven leaflets. The seeds ripen by late summer. Good seed crops are produced every two to three years.

Pop Ash (*F. caroliniana*)

Pop ash is the smallest ash native to Florida, rarely exceeding 40 feet in height. It often has multiple trunks. Pop ash is widely and commonly distributed in wet soil habitats from north Florida to the edge of the Everglades. It frequently grows with cypress (*Taxodium* spp.) in standing

Pop ash (*Fraxinus caroliniana*). Photo by the author.

water. Leaves are composed of five leaflets. Because it is a rather weak tree, it does not provide the same wildlife cover value as other members of this genus. Large, dependable crops of seeds are produced annually.

Green Ash/Pumpkin Ash (*F. pennsylvanica*)

Green ash is a common component of northern forests, but in Florida it is found mostly in moist to wet forest habitats in the north and north central regions. In appearance, this tree greatly resembles white ash. One easily observed difference is that the undersides of its leaves are greenish. The seeds are produced in good numbers annually. Though green ash is an adaptable tree, white ash is a better choice for typical upland landscape settings. If you are landscaping a retention pond, lake, or other low-lying area, however, green ash is an attractive overstory addition.

Green ash (*Fraxinus pennsylvanica*). Photo by Shirley Denton, with permission.

Bald and Pond Cypress

Cypresses (*Taxodium* spp.) are the signature trees of southern forested wetlands. Tall and picturesque, they dominate these systems and play a vital role in their function. They are large, long-lived deciduous trees with broad trunks and scaly, reddish brown bark. Some estimates age our oldest trees at more than 800 years. And, though they take many years to reach a mature height of 80 feet or more, cypresses grow rather quickly during their first decade and initiate flower and fruit production within about 15 years. They have a rather pyramidal shape when young, but older trees acquire a flattened crown. Under typical wetland conditions, these trees also produce knees: raised structures from surface roots that seemingly assist in supplying oxygen to the tree. Because saturated soils are low in oxygen, knees allow these large trees to get the oxygen they need to grow and prosper under conditions that would kill most other species. Cypresses grown in unsaturated soils (like most yards) generally do not develop knees. The broad, strong branches provide home sites for many species of wildlife. Cypresses are dioecious. The cones produced on female trees provide seeds that are eaten by some birds and small mammals, but good seed production occurs only every three or four years. Although some taxonomists consider all cypresses in Florida varieties of a single species, recent taxonomic research indicates that two forms are distinct. Cypresses may be the state's signature wetland trees, but they are very adaptable to upland sites and can be used effectively in home landscapes with typical soil and moisture conditions. Use cypresses as shade trees or in a mixed planting along the shores of ponds and seasonally flooded areas.

Pond Cypress (*T. ascendens*)

Pond cypress is characterized by needlelike leaves extending upward from the branches. This gives pond cypress a very distinctive, almost pinelike appearance and one very different from that of bald cypress. Because of the shape of its leaves, pond cypress provides less wildlife cover than bald cypress. Pond cypress generally occupies different habitats than bald cypress. Under natural conditions, it is found primarily in wet depressions adjacent to lakes, ponds, and other still water. It is well adapted to areas

Pond cypress (*Taxodium ascendens*). Photo by the author.

where water depths of 4 to 6 feet occur for extended periods, and it will grow in saturated shallow soils over limestone. In such shallow soils, it is often stunted and twisted. Pond cypress is not the best choice for typical home landscapes, but it is preferred for use in and around the edges of retention ponds, lakes, and other wet areas where water stands for long periods.

Bald Cypress (*T. distichum*)

Bald cypress is the species familiar to most and the one most widely planted. Unlike the pond cypress, it is characterized by short, feathery leaves. In other physical respects, the two species are similar. Bald cypress

Bald cypress (*Taxodium distichum*). Photo by the author.

normally grows near moving water, especially along the low banks of streams and sloughs and in the floodplains and backwaters of seasonally flooded waterways. Bald cypress is a good choice for home landscaping in a typical yard setting and provides better wildlife cover than pond cypress.

Bays

The bay family is a large family of plants, distributed worldwide. Many are economically important because of their fragrant wood and leaves and/or their berrylike fruit, which normally have a fleshy outer pulp rich in oils and a hard inner seed. Non-native members of this family include the cinnamon (*Cinnamomum zeylandicum*), true bay laurel (*Laurus nobilis*), camphor (*Cinnamomum camphora*), and avocado (*Persea americana*). The bays are especially well suited to coastal plantings as they have a high tolerance of salt. Our native species (except the sassafras, discussed later) are monoecious evergreen trees. Although extremely hardy, they

Lancewood (*Ocotea coriacea*). Photo by Shirley Denton, with permission.

are relatively slow growing and usually produce no fruit during their first decade. Most serve as larval food for spicebush and palamedes swallowtail butterflies, making them important components of a butterfly garden. One serious problem has arisen in recent years, however, that requires consideration before they are planted in the landscape. A fungal pathogen, laurel wilt, spread by an introduced beetle, threatens to decimate every member of this family unless some means is found to stop its spread. If a cure is not found, our bays may go the same route as the American chestnut nearly a century ago.

Lancewood (*Ocotea coriacea*)

Lancewood is an evergreen tree, 25–30 feet tall, resident to coastal hammocks in south Florida. It is shade tolerant and has some cold tolerance. If planted along the coast, it can be used as far north as south central Florida. Lancewood often has an irregular shape with a narrowly rounded crown. The slender branches do not provide much nesting support, but the large elliptical leaves help give it value as hiding cover. Numerous white flowers may be produced any time between March and September, but spring and late summer peaks occur. The ½-inch, purplish black fruit, held in orange red cups, ripen between late fall and winter. They are eaten by a wide variety of wildlife. This valuable wildlife plant is not regularly available from commercial nurseries, but it should be. It is best used as an understory component of a south Florida hammock planting.

Red Bay (*Persea borbonia*)

Red bay is an extremely adaptable evergreen tree (40–60 feet at maturity) native to a variety of habitats throughout Florida. It is found both in upland forests and on coastal dunes. This tree has an irregular shape and a broad rounded crown. Leathery, bright green oval leaves create good cover, and the branches provide good structure for nesting birds. The leaves can also be substituted for true bay laurel leaves in cooking. The ⅓-inch purple fruit ripen by early fall and are eaten by many wildlife. Red bay is a very useful and attractive tree for a wildlife landscape. It is susceptible to a leaf gall that curls the edges of some of its leaves, but because

Red bay (*Persea borbonia*). Photo by the author.

this does not harm the tree in any way, no action should be taken to try to control it. Red bay can be effectively used as a specimen tree or as part of a larger woodland planting.

Silk Bay (*P. humilis*)

Silk bay is considered a red bay variety by some taxonomists and a separate species by others. Regardless, it has several features that make it distinct. This 30–40-foot tree occurs in deep, well-drained, sandy soil habitats in central and south Florida. The undersides of its leaves are covered with dense copper-colored hairs that give the tree an almost golden appearance in the proper wind and sun conditions. The fruit are often slightly larger than red bay, but in other respects the silk bay differs very little from it. Silk bay should be used only in areas with well-drained soils, but in such a setting, few trees can match its aesthetic character or overall value to wildlife.

Left: Silk bay (*Persea humilis*). Photo by the author.

Above: Swamp bay (*Persea palustris*). Photo by the author.

Swamp Bay (*P. palustris*)

Swamp bay is also very similar to red bay and differs significantly only by the types of habitats it frequents. As its name implies, swamp bay is most often found in wetland forests. It is adaptable, however, and can be quite successfully used in most landscape settings where the soils are not excessively drained. Leaf undersides and stems have a shaggy reddish pubescence without the shiny character of the red bay or the deep copper matting of the silk bay. This is a good tree for wet and seasonally flooded areas.

Beautyberry and Fiddlewood

Beautyberry and fiddlewood belong to the mint family, a large family that includes many species cultivated for their ornamental and aromatic values. Mint leaves contain glands with aromatic oils, and many are used in potpourris and to flavor teas and foods. Mints also have showy aromatic blooms that are excellent nectar sources for butterflies and other pollinating insects. As a rule, the native mints do not provide much cover for nesting wildlife, but they have moderate value as hiding cover when planted in groupings. The species described below provide fruit eaten mostly by birds.

Beautyberry (*Callicarpa americana*)

Beautyberry is a 6-foot deciduous shrub native to a wide variety of upland habitats throughout Florida. It is one of the most adaptable native shrubs, thriving in a wide variety of soil and moisture conditions and from full

sun to shade. It is not tolerant of salt, and its best growth generally occurs in partly sunny locations. The leaves of beautyberry planted in too much sun often turn yellowish and the plants grow slowly, while those grown in deep shade get very leggy and produce few flowers and fruit. Beautyberry has numerous slender, wide-spreading branches and large, rough oval leaves with toothed margins. It is monoecious. Clusters of small pinkish flowers (the flowers are white in white-

Beautyberry (*Callicarpa americana*).
Photo by the author.

fruited forms) bloom along the stems at the leaf nodes in late spring and early summer. Unlike many members of this family, they are not especially attractive to butterflies and are pollinated mostly by bees. Numerous magenta-colored berries, ⅛ inch in diameter, ripen along the stems in the fall. White-fruited forms can also be found and are sometimes available from commercial sources. The fruit are the prettiest feature of this shrub and may remain until late winter if not first eaten by birds or mammals. White-tailed deer sometimes consume the foliage. Beautyberry tolerates regular pruning but is best used in areas where its arching branches have room to spread. Use it in a mixed hedge or as an understory shrub in a partly sunny location.

Fiddlewood (*Citharexylum spinosum*)

Fiddlewood is a shrubby, 25-foot evergreen tree native to coastal hammocks in south central Florida and coastal hammocks and pinelands throughout the southern regions of the state. I have found it cold sensitive and do not recommend its use in areas where below freezing temperatures are likely. The many thin branches, square twigs, and opposite elliptical leaves with orange-colored stems are distinctive. Fiddlewood sheds

Fiddlewood (*Citharexylum spinosum*). Photo by the author.

most of its leaves in late winter as its new leaves appear. It is dioecious. Long racemes of white flowers bloom nearly year-round but are especially abundant in May and June. The flowers are extremely fragrant and attract butterflies and a great diversity of other pollinators. The round, ⅓-inch diameter, reddish brown, sticky fruit ripen on the female plants several months later. Besides its value as a fruit producer, fiddlewood is the larval food plant for the caterpillars of several moths. At times, these can almost defoliate the plants, but they also serve as an important food source for birds and their nestlings. Fiddlewood is not tolerant of salt and seems to grow best in sunny, moist locations.

Birches

Members of the birch family in Florida are deciduous trees with minimal wildlife habitat value. In states to our north, the true birches and

alders provide significant food value during the winter months to browsing species, such as rabbits and white-tailed deer, and to game birds, such as ruffed grouse, that feed heavily on their winter buds and young growth. The birch family is also widely favored by the caterpillars of several butterflies and moths; hence, they have value in the production of caterpillars for birds. But these uses are far less important in Florida. Only two species in the birch family, described below, have value for the wildlife landscape, mostly as cover within mixed forested landscapes. None of the birches are tolerant of salt, and all our species are monoecious.

Blue beech/musclewood (*Carpinus caroliniana*). Photo by the author.

Blue Beech/American Hornbeam/Musclewood/Ironwood (*Carpinus caroliniana*)

Blue beech is a small (to 30 feet) understory tree that occurs naturally in moist woodlands in north and central Florida. Because of its shade tolerance, it can be used effectively beneath taller canopy trees. Blue beech has an attractive blue-gray "muscled" trunk and short-spreading branches. It provides fairly good nesting cover in its branches for small to medium-sized birds, but the ⅓-inch nutlets, which ripen in the fall, are of minor use to birds and small mammals. Good seed crops are produced only every three to five years. Its foliage is of only minor importance to browsing wildlife such as white-tailed deer. This tree can be used in much of the northern two-thirds of Florida, but it does best as an understory tree within a mixed forest setting.

Eastern Hophornbeam (*Ostrya virginiana*)

Eastern hophornbeam is another small tree (to about 40 feet) common to the woodland understory. Its distribution in Florida does not extend south beyond north central Florida, and it does not perform well too far

Hop hornbeam (*Ostrya virginiana*). Photo by the author.

south of its natural range. Its outer bark is somewhat shaggy and aesthetically interesting. It gets its name from its fruiting structures, which look like the hops used in beer production. The ¼-inch nutlets have limited use for some birds and small mammals. They ripen in the fall but often persist on the trees until winter. Hophornbeam provides good nesting and hiding cover.

Blackberries

Blackberries (*Rubus* spp.) are a group of prickly deciduous shrubs in the rose family that provide exceptionally effective wildlife habitat. Regrettably, none of our native species are presently commercially available. Blackberry thickets create excellent cover for rabbits and other small mammals, while the sweet, purple fruit are eagerly eaten by birds and other wildlife. Blackberries produce flowers and fruit on the stems produced the previous year. For this reason, wildlife gardeners should be careful how they prune and cut back only the stems that have already fruited. Although blackberries provide exceptional food and cover for a variety of wildlife, they are often a problem in landscapes because they sucker extensively.

Blackberry (*Rubus* spp). Photo by the author.

This greatly limits their use to all but the most naturalistic settings or to areas where the suckering can be effectively controlled. Blackberries can survive very wet soils, but most prefer sunny locations with good drainage. Four native species occur in Florida; sawtooth blackberry (*R. argutus*), sand blackberry (*R. cuneifolius*), northern dewberry (*R. flagellaris*), and southern dewberry (*R. trivialis*). If you wish to use these species, they are easily propagated from root cuttings or seed.

Black Ironwood

Black ironwood (*Krugiodendron ferreum*) belongs to the buckthorn family, along with the darling plum (*Reynosia septentrionalis*), which is not discussed in this book. It is a 25-foot evergreen tree (sometimes shrubby) native to coastal hammocks in south and south central Florida. Although primarily a component of semitropical hammock forests, black ironwood has some cold tolerance and can be used in south central locations where temperatures do not get below the upper 20s Fahrenheit. It has the distinction of having the densest wood of any North American plant. This and its dark furrowed bark give it its common name. Black ironwood has a rather narrow crown, but its dense branches provide good wildlife cover. Its leaves are oval, dark shiny green, and about two inches long. The inconspicuous

Black ironwood (*Krugiodendron ferreum*). Photo by the author.

greenish flowers are produced mainly during the late spring and early summer. They are extremely fragrant and attract a wide variety of pollinating insects. The ⅓-inch sweet and juicy black fruit ripen by late fall and are especially attractive to birds. Black ironwood grows very slowly and is sometimes difficult to establish. It has low to moderate salt tolerance and does not do well in soils that get inundated by saltwater. This is an exceptionally drought-tolerant native that is best planted as a specimen tree in south Florida landscapes or as part of a mixed hammock landscape throughout its landscaping range. Although it will survive shady conditions, it performs best if located where it will receive direct sun for at least half a day.

Black Walnut

Black walnut (*Juglans nigra*), a member of the hickory family, is the most widespread walnut in North America, but its range in Florida is restricted to fertile woodland areas of the central Panhandle. This beautiful tall tree often exceeds 100 feet in height, and the dense rounded crown and sturdy branches provide good cover. Black walnut is renowned for the quality of its wood and flavor of its oily nuts. These 1¼–2-inch nuts are eaten mostly by squirrels and other woodland rodents because the tough shells are

Black walnut (*Juglans nigra*). Shirley Denton, with permission.

difficult for other animals to open. Black walnut is monoecious. Use black walnut as a specimen tree or as part of a mixed woodland planting.

Blolly

Blolly (*Guapira discolor*) is a member of the four o'clock family, which includes several widely used herbaceous flowers and the bougainvillea (*Bougainvillea* spp.). It is our only member with good wildlife habitat value and is native to coastal woodlands throughout south Florida. It is a relatively slow grower, so it might take quite a few years to reach a good size. At maturity, blolly is 30 feet tall. The broad crown and thick, oval, evergreen leaves enhance its cover value for birds and other wildlife, but the branches are rather weak and widely spaced; therefore, it has rather poor cover value for nesting birds, but good hiding cover characteristics if planted as part of a cluster. Blolly is dioecious. Numerous small green tubular flowers are produced from late spring through the summer. Although not showy, they attract a variety of small pollinators. Flowering is followed several months later by clusters of ⅓-inch bright red fruit on the female trees. A blolly covered with fruit is a very showy plant, but the

Blolly (*Guapira discolor*). Photo by the author.

fruit rarely last long as they are eaten quickly by birds. Blolly has one of the most extended fruiting seasons of any of our native plants. Individual flowers within each cluster develop and bloom over many months, and the individual fruit ripen much the same. Because of this, it is possible that each flower cluster contains everything from undeveloped flower buds to fully ripened fruit. Blolly has good salt tolerance and is adaptable to a wide variety of growing conditions. Although it does not naturally reach west central Florida, I have grown it for more than 20 years in Pinellas County, where it has gone through upper 20-degree Fahrenheit winter temperatures without a sign of damage. As with most south Florida hammock plants, fruit production will be enhanced by giving it at least a half-day of sun.

Blueberries

Although this large family contains some of our most commonly used landscape ornamentals, such as azaleas and rhododendrons (*Rhododendron* spp.), and mountain laurel (*Kalmia latifolia*), it is the native blueberries (*Vaccinium* spp.) and huckleberries (*Gaylussacia* spp.) that are important wildlife plants. These species have numerous white bell-shaped flowers in the spring and round, blue or purple succulent fruit in summer or fall. Blueberries are monoecious but produce better crops when cross-pollinated with a second plant. Some are important commercially as human food. All members require acid soils to prosper and have low to medium-low tolerance to salts. They have extremely fine root systems. Because of this and their slow growth, nursery-grown specimens require many months (or years) to become fully established following planting. Plant blueberries and huckleberries during the summer rainy season, and make sure you provide water during periods of drought for at least the first year after planting. As huckleberries are rarely available from commercial sources, I will limit my descriptions to the true blueberries. Blueberries are a complex group of woody plants with great variation within species. Natural hybrids can occur, and differentiating species can be difficult at times. Blueberries spread by underground runners, but the extent of this differs among species. All produce similar fruit, but not all species are sweet. Most blueberries begin producing fruit while still young, and their crops generally are dependable in years without a severe summer drought. Blueberries also serve as a larval food source for many species of moths and some butterflies. Their foliage is browsed by numerous mammals as well, and is especially attractive to white-tailed deer. A total of six distinct species occur in Florida. Five are described below.

Sparkleberry (*Vaccinium arboreum*)

Sparkleberry is a shrubby deciduous tree that may reach 30 feet in height. Native to north and central Florida, it occurs in a variety of habitats from moist hammocks to sand pine scrubs. It tolerates a broader range of soil pH than other blueberries, but still prefers acidic conditions. Sparkleberry has many aesthetic qualities. Its slender twisting trunk and branches give it form and texture, as does its rust-colored, peeling bark. In spring, the trees are covered in fragrant, bell-shaped blooms that attract a wide variety of butterflies, bees, and other pollinators. By fall, the ¼-inch black fruit are ripe and the leaves have turned red. Although the fruit are a bit bland and not especially good for human consumption, they are readily eaten by wildlife. A fully mature sparkleberry provides nesting cover for

Sparkleberry (*Vaccinium arboreum*). Photo by the author.

songbirds, and specimens planted in a mixed-woodland setting provide good hiding cover. In the southern part of its Florida range, sparkleberry does best when planted in filtered sunlight or where it receives sun for only half the day. In north Florida, it can be effectively used in more open settings and makes a very beautiful specimen plant.

Highbush Blueberry (*V. corymbosum*)

Highbush blueberry is a parent plant of all commercial hybrid blueberries grown in eastern North America. Throughout this range, it is extremely variable, and taxonomists have placed some Florida forms as separate species, most notably *V. elliottii*. For the purposes of this book, I have followed more recent convention and lumped all highbush blueberries under *V. corymbosum*. Highbush blueberry occurs naturally in north and central Florida in a variety of wet to well-drained habitats with acidic

soils. It is a multistemmed deciduous shrub that can reach 12 feet in height. It also may sucker and form small colonies, especially if the ground is disturbed around it. The sweet ¼–⅓-inch berries ripen in early summer and vary in color from powdery blue to black. Few fruit attract the attention of wildlife more than those of this shrub. It also provides some cover value once the plant becomes mature. Highbush blueberry will grow in a shady understory location, but fruit production is greatly enhanced if it receives at least a half-day of sun.

Highbush blueberry (*Vaccinium corymbosum*). Photo by Shirley Denton, with permission.

Little blueberry (*Vaccinium darrowii*) (*left*) and shiny blueberry (*Vaccinium myrsinites*) (*right*). Photo by the author.

Little Blueberry (*V. darrowii*)

Little blueberry is one of two species of dwarf evergreen blueberries that rarely exceed 3 feet in height. It occurs from north to south central Florida in well-drained sandy soils and in seasonally wet pinelands with acidic soils. It spreads by underground suckers and forms localized colonies. Little blueberry has small, blue green leaves. The ¼-inch sweet fruit are powdery blue and ripen during the early summer. Because the fruit are produced in quantities close to the ground, it provides a valuable food source for wildlife such as gopher tortoise, wild turkey, and bobwhite quail. This, and shiny blueberry described next, make excellent ground covers for sunny or partly sunny locations, given the proper pH conditions.

Shiny Blueberry (*V. myrsinites*)

Shiny blueberry is very similar to little blueberry in growth characteristics and distribution, and they often occur together on the same site. Shiny

Deerberry/dangleberry (*Vaccinium stamineum*). Photo by the author.

blueberry, however, has small bright green leaves, and the sweet fruit are shiny black. Both species of dwarf blueberries are widely available in the native plant nursery trade. They can be mixed together as wildlife ground cover or used separately. Because of their low stature, they do not provide much cover value and are best used planted in masses or colonies.

Deerberry/Dangleberry (*V. stamineum*)

Deerberry is a deciduous shrub that can reach 15 feet in height. It has an open growth habit that enhances its ornamental value but reduces its ability to provide very effective wildlife cover. Deerberry occurs mostly in the understory of open woodlands with well-drained sandy soils. It ranges from north to south central Florida. In the spring, it produces a mass of open, bell-shaped flowers that hang from the branches on pronounced stalks. The mature, ⅓–½-inch fruit vary in color from pink, amber, and reddish to blue and dark purple. They are sweet and readily eaten by wildlife after they ripen in summer. This species is best planted in an open woodland setting or at the outer edge of a shaded hammock planting. Of the five species described, it is the least available commercially.

Bumelias

Although taxonomists rather recently revised this group and put them under a different genus name (*Sideroxylon*), I prefer to continue using bumelia as the common name. Bumelias are sometimes referred to as "buckthorns," but they are in the Sapotaceae and should not be confused with true buckthorns in the Rhamnaceae family. Bumelias are small trees or shrubs with dense, strong wood and often with thorns or thorny spurs along their branches. Different species are found throughout Florida in different habitat types. Their branches produce good cover, and their small blackish fruit are an excellent food source for many songbirds and other wildlife. I have a particular fondness for bumelias, but it is a somewhat confusing group for plant taxonomists. Florida is home to numerous species, all of which are excellent choices for the wildlife landscape. Regrettably, most are not commercially available, and some are difficult to grow. I have generally limited the discussion below to those species that are commercially available, but I have included several rarely offered species that are especially useful.

Alachua Buckthorn (*Sideroxylon alachuense*)

Alachua buckthorn is a little-known and poorly described shrubby tree that occurs around the Gainesville area as well as a few other forested habitats in northeast and north central Florida and extreme southeastern Georgia. Although it has a very limited natural range, it is fairly adaptable and can be grown throughout much of the north and central portions of the state. Alachua buckthorn has stout branches and very dense foliage when grown in mostly sunny locations. The branches are armed with stout, short spur shoots. These characteristics make it especially good as hiding cover for birds and other wildlife. The undersides of the oval, tardily deciduous leaves are silvery pubescent, and they shimmer when the wind blows. Alachua buckthorn grows naturally in moderate shade in the understory of moist-soil forests and in soils that are slightly alkaline. This seemingly rare plant grows to about 9 feet tall. Flowering occurs in the spring, and the ⅔-inch fruit ripen by late summer. Although this bumelia can be grown successfully as an understory shrub in a mixed-forest

Alachua buckthorn (*Sideroxylon ala-chuense*). Photo by the author.

landscape setting, it performs better when given more light as part of a mixed-shrub hedge or thicket.

Saffron Plum (*S. celastrinum*)

Saffron plum is a 20-foot evergreen tree native to the southern half of Florida. It has some cold hardiness but should not be used in locations where temperatures fall below the mid-20s Fahrenheit. Its short trunk has a checkered and deeply fissured bark, and its crown is dense and rounded. Branches are slender and spreading, armed with short, rigid spines. All the characteristics mentioned above make this plant excellent for providing wildlife cover. Highly aromatic, whitish flowers bloom throughout the year, but most often in the spring and fall. These attract a great many insect pollinators. The ¾-inch fruit ripen approximately three months later

Saffron plum (*Sideroxylon celastrinum*). Photo by the author.

and provide large amounts of wildlife food. Saffron plum is salt tolerant and adaptable to soil and light conditions, although it is most abundant in moist-soil habitats near the coast. This bumelia is especially slow growing and takes many years to produce flowers and fruit. Despite this, it is one of my favorite natives and worth the time and patience. Saffron plum is best used as an accent plant where its fragrant flowers can be fully appreciated. If used as part of a mixed-species planting, make sure it gets enough light to flower and set fruit.

Mastic (*Sideroxylon foetidissimum*). Photo by the author.

Mastic (*S. foetidissimum*)

Mastic is a broad-crowned evergreen tree native to south Florida hammocks that may reach 60 feet in height. It has some cold tolerance and occurs in coastal woodlands as far north as Cape Canaveral on the east coast. The wide oval leaves are yellowish green with wavy margins and are clustered at the branch tips. Both the leaves and bark have a strong fetid odor. Mastic provides good hiding cover, but only moderate nesting cover because many of its branches are long and thin. Light yellow, unpleasantly fragrant flowers bloom mostly in midsummer and attract many pollinating insects. Large numbers of yellow 1-inch "plums" ripen from February to March. They are eaten and dispersed by a variety of wildlife. Mastic has good tolerance for salt spray, but much less so for inundation of its roots by saltwater. This is an exceptionally stately tree that makes a wonderful shade tree for south Florida landscapes. It also is effectively used as a canopy tree within a mixed south Florida hammock landscape.

Wooly Buckthorn/Gum Bumelia (*S. lanuginosum*)

Wooly buckthorn is another wonderful bumelia that is rarely offered in the commercial nursery trade. I include it here in hopes that this might someday change. Wooly buckthorn is an irregularly shaped, deciduous shrubby tree that may reach 30 feet in height. Most common in the understory of sandy woodlands, it occurs throughout north and central Florida in a variety of inland and near-coastal habitats. The dark outer bark is deeply furrowed and the branches are thin and spreading, with very sparse thorniness. This and its somewhat open aspect provide only moderate wildlife cover value, less than most others described in this text. Despite this, wooly buckthorn is aesthetically interesting and adds character to a wildlife landscape. The undersides of the oval-shaped leaves are densely covered with coppery colored "wool," and this sets the plant apart when used in a mixed-woodland planting. The small white flowers in the spring produce large numbers of sweet, ⅖-inch fruit in the fall eaten by songbirds and small mammals. Wooly buckthorn makes a very interesting accent plant or is effectively incorporated into the understory of an open-woodland planting. It has some tolerance of salt spray, but little tolerance of saltwater inundation.

Wooly buckthorn (*Sideroxylon lanuginosum*). Photo by the author.

Willow Bustic (*S. salicifolium*)

Willow bustic is a 30-foot evergreen tree native to south Florida hammock woodlands. Its cold tolerance is poorly known and it should, therefore, not be used too far north of its natural range. It has an upright narrow crown, and the branches are rather slender and arching. The willowlike leaves tend to hang downward from the stems, and the overall nature of this species makes it only moderately good for hiding cover and poor for nesting cover. Willow bustic is a good food plant, however. Many small white flowers bloom for a several-week period between February and May. They are fragrant and attract a variety of butterflies and other pollinating insects. These are followed in the summer by many ¼-inch purplish black fruit. Willow bustic is the larval host for several moth caterpillars, including the ello sphinx moth. These caterpillars sometimes nearly defoliate the trees, but they supply needed food for adult birds and their nestlings.

Willow bustic (*Sideroxylon salicifolium*). Photo by the author.

Willow bustic is tolerant of a variety of growing conditions, including a moderate tolerance of salt. It performs best, however, in ample sunshine.

Tough Bumelia/Silver Buckthorn (*S. tenax*)

Tough bumelia is the most widely grown species of this group and one of the most beautiful. Often an irregular, tardily deciduous shrub or small tree up to 20 feet tall, tough bumelia is native to coastal and interior scrublands throughout Florida, except the Panhandle. It is exceptionally drought tolerant but will not prosper in soils with poor drainage or that retain water for even short periods. This is a bumelia with greatly varying characteristics. Most specimens have stout crooked branches with some thorns and numerous thorny spur shoots. Specimens of this type rarely produce a typical trunk and remain as dense shrubs. Treelike forms also occur. All forms have dark green linear leaves with a dense coppery pubescence covering the undersides. The uneven aspect and beautiful foliage make this plant stand out. Shrubby forms can be very effectively used to create thickets. Treelike forms make superb specimen plants. Flowering occurs in late spring, and the ½-inch fruit ripen by fall.

Silver buckthorn (*Sideroxylon tenax*). Photo by the author.

Cedars

This large family of evergreens includes two species of trees with great wildlife landscape value. Both have scalelike leaves, and the dense foliage provides excellent cover for screening purposes and for wildlife. Additionally, both have great salt tolerance and are very adaptable to soil conditions.

Atlantic White Cedar (*Chamaecyparis thyoides*)

Atlantic white cedar is a long-lived but very slow-growing tree that may eventually reach 60 feet at maturity. Dwarf forms are available. Within Florida, it is restricted largely to acidic freshwater swamps and occurs naturally only in north and north central counties. It is much more adaptable than this natural distribution might suggest and can be grown well into central Florida in a wide variety of soils and typical landscape settings. This tree does not perform well as an understory plant. Atlantic white cedar has many attributes for the wildlife landscape. Its dense, nonspiny foliage produces excellent cover and is eaten by white-tailed deer and other browsing mammals. Several species of butterfly and moth caterpillars also use it as a larval food source, but this use is less important in the southern portion of its landscape range. Atlantic white cedar is monoecious and produces its small bluish purple cones at a very early age, sometimes as early

Atlantic white cedar (*Chamaecyparis thyoides*). Photo by the author.

as three years. Each cone contains 5–16 very small winged seeds that are released during the fall. The seeds have very limited value as wildlife food, but are consumed by some songbirds and small mammals.

Southern Red Cedar (*Juniperus virginiana*; syn. *J. silicicola*)

Southern red cedar is an extremely adaptable species that occurs naturally throughout north and central Florida in nearly every type of growing condition, including coastal habitats. In some areas it is a major component of riverine swamp forests, but in other locations it can be common in coastal dune forests and in open dry fields. This long-lived but slow-growing tree may eventually reach 60 feet in height, and it retains its somewhat pyramidal shape throughout. As the tree matures, its distinctive reddish, scaly bark enhances its ornamental character. Young red cedars make excellent screening hedges, but older trees lose their lower branches and form tall straight trunks. Southern red cedar is one of the best native trees for wildlife cover because of its dense, somewhat spiny foliage. Its strong branches provide structure for the nests of many songbirds. Southern red cedar also excels as a food plant. It is dioecious, so only the female trees produce the ⅓-inch bluish gray fruit, which ripen in the fall. Cedar fruit are eaten by a variety of birds, but fruit production varies each year. The foliage is not important to browsing wildlife, but several species of moth and butterfly caterpillars consume it, making it somewhat useful to

Southern red cedar (*Juniperus virginiana*). Photo by the author.

birds that eat caterpillars. Southern red cedar should not be planted in landscapes near hawthorns or apples because red cedars serve as a host for cedar-apple rust disease, which kills these other plants.

Cherries and Plums

Cherries and plums belong to the genus *Prunus* and are members of the rose family. Our species are either shrubs or trees. Although their fruits differ somewhat in size and shape, all are recognized by their abundant showy white flowers in the spring and their round juicy fruit that surrounds a stonelike inner pit. The flowers are exceptionally attractive to butterflies and other pollinators. Cherries and plums are monoecious. None of our species are thorny, but several native plums have thornlike spur shoots that greatly enhance their wildlife cover value. Some species sucker and can produce dense thickets. Care should be taken in using these species in the home landscape or they will ultimately become difficult to control. The fruit of all species are especially attractive to wildlife that widely disperse the seeds in their droppings. Because of this, many species rapidly colonize open ground. The wilted foliage of cherries and plums is toxic to livestock, so they should not be planted in areas where they might be browsed. As a member of the rose family, cherries and plums are the host of a great many butterfly and moth caterpillars. At times, they can be heavily infested with these larvae, becoming significant magnets to various songbirds that rely on the caterpillars for themselves and their nestlings. Most species are restricted to north and central Florida; only a few are salt tolerant. Seven species occur naturally in Florida, but only some are commercially available and good choices for the wildlife landscape.

Chickasaw Plum (*P. angustifolia*)

Chickasaw plum is one of the toughest and most adaptable members of this genus for use in Florida. Generally a single-trunk, shrubby, deciduous tree, this plum grows rapidly to 20 feet, maturing at an early age. Chickasaw plum occurs throughout north and central Florida in sandy,

Chickasaw plum (*Prunus angustifolia*). Photo by the author.

well-drained soils. It is adaptable to most sunny upland conditions but has fairly low tolerance of salt and should not be used in the most southern portions of the state. Its dense strong branches provide ideal structure for many nesting songbirds and excellent hiding cover for many wildlife species. Aesthetically, it has few peers in the spring. Numerous clusters of fragrant white flowers envelop the tree in February and March. These, in turn, attract large numbers of butterflies, bees, and other pollinators. By late June or early July, the flowers have developed into round, reddish to reddish yellow ½-inch plums. Although too large for the smaller songbirds, they are relished by larger birds and many mammals. They are also good for making jelly. Though Chickasaw plum is an excellent addition to the wildlife landscape, it has one major drawback that must be considered prior to incorporating it into a mixed planting: mature plants frequently spread by root suckers. This is especially problematic if the roots are cut by activities such as digging and planting within the dripline of established specimens. Root suckers can be controlled by mowing or pruning the suckers, or by judicious use of herbicides—taking care only to treat the suckers themselves. If you use this beautiful native, try to plant the rest of your landscape around it at the same time—before the roots spread out. The more you disturb the area around this tree, the more it will sucker and spread.

Cherry Laurel/Laurel Cherry (*P. caroliniana*)

Cherry laurel is an evergreen, narrow-crowned, 30-foot tree native to a variety of habitats throughout most of Florida, except the extreme southern counties. It has some salt tolerance and occurs inland in both moist and well-drained soils. Because it is exceptionally adaptable, cherry laurel can be used in a wide variety of settings. It is even sometimes used as a hedge because it tolerates regular shearing. As a wildlife plant, it is very good at providing both cover and food. Small racemes of white flowers bloom in early spring. The ½-inch shiny black fruit ripen by late summer but persist into the winter if they are uneaten. Often, this is one of the last fruits left in the landscape during the dead of winter when migratory birds such as American robins and cedar waxwings are looking for fuel before heading north. At such times, a cherry laurel becomes a magnet for these birds. Cherry laurel can be used as a specimen tree, but it is equally

Cherry laurel (*Prunus caroliniana*). Photo by the author.

effective when planted in the background of a mixed woodland where it will get some direct sunlight. Although it will tolerate a lot of shade, its best growth occurs in open, fertile sites. Because cherry laurel fruit is so widely consumed by wildlife, it often becomes established on its own from bird droppings and from the feeding behavior of gray squirrels. If a cherry laurel is in the neighborhood, you will quickly learn which areas of your landscape are the preferred wildlife roosting spots. Pull your volunteer seedlings out before they get too large and more difficult to remove. This species also tends to root sucker.

West Indian Cherry/Myrtle Cherry (*P. myrtifolia*)

West Indian cherry is a tropical evergreen tree native to south Florida hammock woodlands that reaches 25 feet. The large glossy leaves have an undulating margin and no teeth. White racemes of very fragrant flowers bloom in November and December, and the ⅓-inch black cherries ripen in early summer. West Indian cherry is an adaptable tree and can be used in most south Florida locations. It does not have especially high tolerance for salt or shade, so it is best planted in sunnier locations out of

West Indian cherry (*Prunus myrtifolia*). Photo by Roger Hammer, with permission.

direct salt spray. As a wildlife plant, it provides both food and cover in good measure. This beautiful south Florida native is only occasionally offered commercially, but is an excellent choice for the right setting.

Black Cherry (*P. serotina*)

Black cherry is another species common to a wide variety of habitats throughout north and central Florida. It is excellent at tolerating the shade of mature woodlands, but it will also thrive and rapidly colonize disturbed fields and fence rows. It has some tolerance of salt and can be grown in

many locations where other plums and cherries would fail. Black cherry is a deciduous, narrow-crowned tree that reaches 60 feet or more in height. The bark of mature specimens is nearly black, and the dense foliage is a bright shiny green. In the fall, the leaves turn shades of yellow, orange, and red, producing a wonderful show of color. Black cherry offers ideal conditions for nesting birds and other wildlife within its many strong branches. Long racemes of fragrant white flowers bloom in the spring.

Black cherry (*Prunus serotina*). Photo by the author.

Numerous ⅓-inch purplish black fruit ripen by summer and are highly prized by many wildlife species. Although black cherry produces fruit annually, large crops occur only about every three years. This is an extremely adaptable and excellent wildlife tree for the northern third of Florida. Use it as a specimen tree or in a partly sunny to full-sun location in an open woodland setting. As with the cherry laurel, described above, birds will disperse the seeds of black cherry widely, and seedlings may need to be controlled. Black cherry is the host plant for a great many native butterflies and some nuisance moths, such as tent caterpillars and fall webworms. This is an added benefit for the wildlife gardener looking to feed both birds and butterflies, but it can be aesthetically displeasing to some.

Flatwoods Plum/Hog Plum (*P. umbellata*)

Flatwoods plum is sometimes called the "forgotten" plum, because it has been largely overlooked or ignored. It is a beautiful and useful 20-foot deciduous tree that deserves far more use and recognition. Native to both pine and hardwood woodlands of average drainage in much of Florida, except the extreme southern counties, it is sometimes confused with the Chickasaw plum, described above. The differences between the two species are many, however. Flatwoods plum is a somewhat-crooked single-trunk tree. It is often taller than it is broad. The leaf blades are flat, not

Flatwoods plum (*Prunus umbellata*). Photo by the author.

slightly folded. The white flowers bloom in late spring, often several weeks later than those of Chickasaw plum, and the somewhat smaller, ½-inch red to yellow fruit ripen several weeks later in summer. Flatwoods plum is not salt tolerant and is less commonly armed with thorny spur shoots. This plum is best used as an understory tree in a woodland landscape where it receives filtered or partial sun. If planted in full sun, it grows best in locations that receive a bit of extra moisture. Flatwoods plum almost never suckers and is far easier to control in a landscape than Chickasaw plum. Although this species is becoming more common in the nursery trade, it may take a little searching to find it. It is well worth the search.

Coco Plums

This family contains only two species in eastern North America, both occurring in Florida and both with value in the wildlife landscape.

Coco Plum (*Chrysobalanus icaco*)

Coco plum occurs as two distinct forms, both commercially available. One form is an upright shrub with a rounded crown that can reach 15 feet in height. The other is a horizontal woody ground cover that rarely stands taller than 12 to 18 inches. Both forms have rounded glossy evergreen

Coco plum (*Chrysobalanus icaco*). Photo by the author.

foliage that is aesthetically attractive. Coco plum occurs throughout south Florida in moist-soil communities but is adaptable to much drier soils. It has high salt tolerance and will tolerate cold temperatures into the upper 20s Fahrenheit for short periods. Coco plum is an excellent wildlife plant for regions of the state that do not regularly freeze. Upright forms are good wildlife cover, and both forms are superb food producers. The small, greenish flowers attract many pollinating insects, while the "plums" are round, about ½ inch in diameter, dark purple (sometimes whitish), and sweet tasting. Many species of wildlife relish them, but their relatively large size reduces their value for small birds. Fruit are produced nearly year-round. In addition to their ornamental and wildlife value, the fruit were an important food source for the Seminole and Miccosukee Indians and are still used in jellies and preserves.

Gopher Apple
(*Licania michauxii*)

Gopher apple is a woody, evergreen ground cover, native to sunny, well-drained habitats throughout Florida. In most situations, it rarely exceeds 12 inches in height, and each stem is rather thin. Over time it slowly spreads to cover wide areas of open ground. Gopher apple blooms in the summer, and the 1-inch white fruit ripen by late fall. The flowers attract a wide variety of pollinating insects, but the large fruit are of interest mostly to mammals and gopher tortoises. This plant is best used as a ground cover in open sandy areas to replace grasses or other ground covers with less wildlife value.

Gopher apple (*Licania michauxii*).
Photo by the author.

Coffees

This is one of the largest families of flowering plants in the world and includes many non-natives that are commercially or horticulturally important, such as the true coffee tree (*Coffea arabica*), gardenia (*Gardenia* spp.), ixora (*Ixora* spp.), and pentas (*Pentas lanceolata*). Most of our native species are not especially important wildlife cover plants but excel at producing fruit and flowers. The family includes the native firebush (*Hamelia patens*) and white indigoberry (*Randia aculeata*), discussed under separate headings, as well as three species of wild coffee (*Psychotria* spp.), discussed below. The wild coffees are monoecious evergreen shrubs found in peninsular Florida. Although their use may be extended to portions of the panhandle, none of our species are naturally found there. Wild coffees are characterized by large, elliptical leaves with noticeably impressed veins and abundant clusters of small white flowers attractive to certain butterflies (especially the zebra heliconian), bees, and many other pollinators. The flowers are followed by clusters of elliptical, ¼–⅓-inch bright red fruit. The flowers can bloom throughout the year but are most abundant in the spring. The fruit ripen mostly in the late fall and winter. Florida's native species are weakly branched and provide cover mostly in the understory and when massed. They tolerate dense shade and occur mostly in moist wooded habitats.

Bahama coffee (*Psychotria ligustrifolia*). Photo by the author.

Bahama Coffee (*P. ligustrina*)

Bahama coffee is a 4-foot species native only to extreme south Florida. It has reasonable cold tolerance, however, and specimens I planted in Pinellas County more than 20 years ago have thrived despite occasional freezing temperatures. Bahama coffee is similar in appearance to the far more common shiny coffee, but the leaves are not as noticeably wrinkled, and the fruit is a bit more dull red in color. Bahama coffee has some tolerance of salt spray, but little tolerance of saltwater at its roots. Like all members of this genus, it is best used as a mass planting in the understory of shaded woodland landscapes. In this setting, it will provide evergreen cover for ground-dwelling wildlife and sustained flowering and fruiting throughout the year.

Shiny-leaved Coffee (*P. nervosa*)

Shiny-leaved coffee is the most commercially available and widely used species of this genus. It is a variable shrub that occurs from coastal hammocks in northeast Florida throughout regions to the south. At the northern end of its range, it is a 1–2-foot ground cover, but in south Florida it is more likely to reach 6 feet or more. A dwarf form is commercially available that stays 1–2 feet regardless of growing conditions. Shiny-leaved

Shiny-leaved coffee (*Psychotria nervosa*). Photo by the author.

coffee has exceptionally attractive foliage. The deep green leaves are decidedly wrinkled on the upper surface and give this plant a unique appearance. In other respects, it is very similar to Bahama coffee and can be used in similar landscape settings.

Softleaf Coffee (*P. sulzneri*)

Softleaf coffee grows in hammocks throughout the southern half of peninsular Florida. It is very distinct from the other two coffees described above, being somewhat lanky and much less dense. Often a shrub 3–4 feet tall, softleaf coffee has rather weak branches and thin drooping leaves. The leaves are grayish green with a velvety sheen and only slightly wrinkled. Despite some of its limitations as cover, softleaf coffee produces great amounts of bright-red fruit that are eagerly eaten by a wide assortment of wildlife. This species has some tolerance to salt spray, but does not do well when inundated by saltwater.

Softleaf coffee (*Psychotria sulzneri*). Photo by the author.

Dogwoods

Dogwoods (*Cornus* spp.) are deciduous shrubs or small trees, prized for their ornamental flowers and rich fall color. They produce flowers that attract a wide variety of pollinating insects and succulent fruit eaten by many species of wildlife. There are several dogwoods native to Florida, but only two are commercially available and adaptable to many landscape settings. Neither are tolerant of salt, and both are monoecious.

Flowering Dogwood (*C. florida*)

Flowering dogwood is one of the most widely planted ornamental native trees in the south. In Florida, flowering dogwood occurs mostly in well-drained, slightly acidic, sandy soils in north and central counties. It should not be attempted much south of its natural range, and care should be taken to use only specimens raised from Florida stock, as others may not perform well in this climate. It is most effectively used as a specimen tree or as an understory component of a mixed-woodland landscape. At maturity, this tree might reach 40 feet in height, but most often remains at about 25 feet. Despite its popularity as a landscape tree, many gardeners

Flowering dogwood (*Cornus florida*). Photo by the author.

are unaware that it is also a valuable wildlife plant. The branches of this graceful tree help support the nests of songbirds. The small flowers, surrounded by large showy bracts, bloom in early spring. By fall, the numerous ½-inch, red, egg-shaped fruit are ripe and eagerly consumed by many birds and mammals.

Swamp Dogwood (*C. foemina*)

Swamp dogwood is much less frequently used, but has much to offer the home landscape. As its name implies, it occurs naturally in wetland habitats but will adapt to drier conditions once established. It has the widest natural range of any of our native dogwoods and can be used nearly statewide with good results. Swamp dogwood is a multitrunk tree or dense shrub that rarely exceeds 15 feet in height. Its best landscape uses are along pond and wetland margins or within the outer canopy of a mixed-woodland planting, where its flowers can be admired. Although not nearly as showy as its better known relative, described above, swamp dogwood produces many clusters of white flowers in the spring. By midsummer, these

Swamp dogwood (*Cornus foemina*). Photo by the author.

have ripened into ¼-inch pale blue fruit. Swamp dogwood fruit do not all ripen at the same time, so food production is extended over many weeks. Ripe fruit are rapidly eaten, but those that remain are not held long before shriveling and dropping to the ground. Although swamp dogwood is an excellent food plant, its weak branches and relatively open character create only moderate cover.

Elderberries

Elderberries are members of the honeysuckle family, which includes another important group of wildlife plants, the viburnums (*Viburnum* spp.), also described in this book. Current taxonomy now places all the elderberries east of the Mississippi River into one species, described below. All elderberries are monoecious.

Elderberry (*Sambucus nigra* ssp. *canadensis*, syn. *S. canadensis, S. simpsonii*)

Elderberry is an extremely common shrub or small tree, native to a wide variety of upland and wetland habitats throughout Florida. It will tolerate nearly every type of growing condition, but seems to thrive best where it gets plenty of sun and a bit of extra moisture. Although single specimens have little cover value, elderberries will sucker to form thickets of good cover if left alone. Elderberries can be difficult to contain within the home landscape because of their tendency to spread by root suckers. For this reason, their introduction into a home landscape should be carefully considered. There is no argument that elderberries have great value to wildlife. Flowering and fruit production will occur throughout the year in areas where winter freezes do not interrupt them. Elderberry flowers are magnets for a great many pollinating insects, and these in turn provide food for many insect-eating songbirds. The flowers are quickly followed by vast quantities of ⅕-inch edible dark purple fruit especially attractive to birds and small mammals. Deer browse on the foliage. In north Florida, elderberry is a deciduous shrub, but in south Florida it is evergreen. In this setting, it is almost always in fruit and flower. Elderberry has little

Elderberry (*Sambucus nigra* spp. *canadensis*). Photo by the author.

salt tolerance. It can be used effectively as an accent plant or as part of a mixed-species thicket. Although this species will grow well in partial shade, flower and fruit production are maximized in settings where it gets at least a half-day of sunshine.

Elms

The elms are a medium-sized family of deciduous trees and shrubs distributed mostly in temperate regions of the Northern Hemisphere. They are widely used as shade trees in developed landscapes, and their relatively rapid growth, tall straight trunks, and spreading crowns give them great ornamental value. Elms are most common in fertile moist-soil habitats but are adaptable to most growing conditions. They have simple, asymmetrical oval leaves with toothed margins and pointed tips. Elms also are characterized by their pyramidal shape. Few of our native trees are better at providing nesting structure for songbirds. All our species are monoecious. Small, nonshowy flowers are produced mostly in the spring before leaf-out, and they attract a variety of small pollinators that also provide a food source for migratory songbirds heading north. The fruit are dry seeds enclosed in a papery wing. Depending on the species and the time of year the seeds ripen, elms can be an important source of food for songbirds and small mammals. Seeds of the spring-fruiting species tend to be used more, because they ripen at a time when other foods are scarce. Good seed production generally occurs only every two to three years. Elms have very little tolerance of salt spray and are not good choices for coastal areas. Four species occur in Florida, but only two are widely distributed and commercially available. Use elms as shade trees in the northern half of the state. They can also be effectively used as a canopy tree in a mixed-forest landscape. Although relatively fast growing and quick to mature, elms are relatively long lived.

Winged Elm (*U. alata*)

Winged elm is a large (to 100 feet), distinctive tree native to upland woodland habitats in north and central Florida. Named for the corky wings that often form on its limbs and trunk, this is one tree that is nearly as attractive in the winter without leaves as it is during the rest of the year. Winged elms have small leaves that turn yellow in the fall. Flowering occurs in late winter, and the ¼-inch seeds ripen by late March. This drought-tolerant tree has a wide range of landscape uses and is an excellent choice for its great wildlife value. Thankfully, it is widely available.

Winged elm (*Ulmus alata*). Photo by the author.

American Elm (*U. americana*)

American elm (*Ulmus americana*).
Photo by the author.

American elm is a large (about 70 feet) tree native to moist hardwood forest habitats throughout Florida, except the Keys and the extreme southern peninsula. This species has been devastated by Dutch elm disease in northern states, but this disease has not spread to Florida and our trees have continued to thrive. American elms have rather large leaves that turn a rich yellow in the fall. Flowering occurs in the early spring and the ⅓-inch seeds ripen about one month later. American elm is an adaptable tree that will thrive in most landscape settings, except extremely droughty soils or areas immediately on the coast. It is also more tolerant of shade than the winged elm. This tree is widely available.

Figs

Florida is besieged by a host of aggressive non-native figs (*Ficus* spp.) that threaten natural areas in the south. While these species are very harmful to our ecology and should never be planted, we have two species of native figs with great value to wildlife. Only one is widely available from commercial sources.

Strangler Fig (*F. aurea*)

Strangler fig is a native of south and south central Florida woodlands. As its name implies, it often starts out by sprouting in the branches of other trees, after being deposited in bird droppings. Over time, these seedlings send their roots downward toward the soil, and the developing tree slowly engulfs its host. After a few years, all that remains is the fig. Strangler fig is a rapidly growing tree that eventually reaches a mature height of 60 feet. It often has multiple trunks and, like most figs, produces aerial roots that soon become "trunklike." As such, this is not a plant for the more traditional landscape setting. Strangler fig is best used as part of a dense forest hammock planting where its large size and sprawling habit are not a problem. Despite its drawbacks, strangler fig has numerous attributes that make it a good addition to a wildlife landscape. It is monoecious. The small ¾-inch figs are relished by birds and small mammals. Flowering and fruit production occur nearly year-round. The flowers do not attract a wide assortment of pollinators, but the foliage provides a larval food source for one of Florida's most beautiful butterflies; the ruddy daggerwing. Strangler fig has thick, elliptical, evergreen leaves that provide cover in the broad-spreading canopy. The stout branches also serve as good nest sites for various songbirds.

Strangler fig (*Ficus aurea*).
Photo by the author.

Firebush

Our native firebush (*Hamelia patens*) is a fast-growing evergreen shrub that may reach 12 feet in height in south Florida, where freezing temperatures are uncommon. Its range extends, however, to south central Florida hammocks, and in these locations it is generally much smaller. Firebush is an excellent shrub for areas protected from harsh winter temperatures. It will freeze to the ground if temperatures dip below 32 degrees Fahrenheit for even a few minutes, but will resprout rapidly as soon as temperatures rise above freezing. You can use this plant in areas where temperatures are moderate (even into north Florida), but extended periods of below-freezing conditions will kill it. It has some tolerance of salt spray but does not do well in areas frequently inundated by saltwater. It is also fairly drought tolerant but greatly prefers soils with additional moisture. It will become stunted and eventually die if planted in soils that are too droughty or too infertile. Firebush is a rather weak-limbed monoecious shrub, and it provides little structure for nesting wildlife. In areas where it does not regularly freeze, its dense foliage provides hiding cover. The real value of this plant to the wildlife gardener is its blooms and the fruit that follows. During most months of the year, firebush is covered by numerous scarlet

Firebush (*Hamelia patens*). Photo by the author.

orange flowers and dark purple fruit. The flowers attract hummingbirds and butterflies like few other native plants, and the large continuous crop of ¼-inch dark purple fruit attracts many birds and other wildlife. Fire-bush is tolerant of a wide range of light, moisture, and soil conditions, though it does best in partial sun in fertile, slightly alkaline soil. It is best used in open locations as an accent plant or at the outer edges of a mixed planting where it gets at least a half-day of sun. Several similar but non-native firebush species are now being sold commercially. Be careful to choose the native one.

Fringetrees

I admit that I have a severe weakness for fringetrees (*Chionanthus* spp.). While they will never be considered a top-tier wildlife landscape plant, I cannot refrain from planting them wherever I reside. The sight of their dense mantle of tasseled white flowers in the late spring is one of my greatest joys of the season, and I look forward to them each year with an-ticipation. Following this show of flowers, they are far less awe inspiring. Fringetrees are small, often multitrunk deciduous trees with a rather open character and relatively weak branches. As such, they do not provide very effective wildlife cover. They are also exceptionally slow growing, adding growth only when they leaf out in the spring. They mature at a very young age, however, and begin blooming within the first five years. Fringetrees are dioecious. Female trees bear large clusters of ½¾-inch purple fruit that ripen by late summer; these are eaten by birds and small mammals. Most taxonomists include two species in Florida's flora, but the pigmy fringetree (*C. pygmaeus*) is quite rare and often unavailable. Neither spe-cies tolerates salt.

Fringetree/Old Man's Beard (*Chionanthus virginicus*)

Fringetree eventually reaches a mature height of about 20 feet. It grows ev-erywhere in the northern two-thirds of Florida and prefers fertile, moist soil. Throughout north Florida, it is often used as a specimen tree, but farther south it seems to perform best only when given protection from full-day sun. For the wildlife landscape, fringetrees should be planted in

Fringetree (*Chionanthus virginicus*). Photo by the author.

mixed-woodland settings as subcanopy trees. Because they are dioecious, take care to plant several to ensure you get pollination and at least one female.

Gumbo Limbo

Gumbo limbo (*Bursera simaruba*) is a widespread south Florida tree tolerant of a variety of growing conditions, including salt spray. Although it is a south Florida native, it will survive winter temperatures that dip for short periods into the upper 20s Fahrenheit. It occurs along the Florida coastline as far north as Pinellas County on the west and Volusia County on the east. It grows rapidly and at maturity may exceed 60 feet in height. With its shiny, copper-colored peeling bark and its rich green foliage, gumbo limbo can be effectively used in a wide variety of landscape

Gumbo limbo (*Bursera simaruba*). Photo by the author.

settings. Although I find it most interesting as a component of a mixed coastal-woodland planting, it will work equally well as a specimen tree or as a tree for shade near the beach. Gumbo limbo has compound leaves that are deciduous for a brief period in late winter at the time its small white flowers appear. These flowers attract a wide assortment of insect pollinators and the songbirds that feed on them. The ½-inch reddish fruit ripen in late fall or early winter and are of moderate value to birds and small mammals. Gumbo limbo is monoecious. The broad canopy provides some cover, but its open nature reduces its value. Gumbo limbo is extremely easy to propagate. Even large branches will root and form new trees when simply shoved into moist sand and left alone.

Hackberries

The hackberries (*Celtis* spp.) are a widely distributed genus within the elm family with both temperate and tropical representatives. They are characterized by rapid growth, early maturity, and a relatively short life span.

Our species are monoecious deciduous trees with exceptional value in the wildlife landscape. Four species occur in Florida, but only one is commercially available and likely to be used. It is discussed below.

Sugarberry (*C. laevigata*)

Sugarberry is a large tree common to moist woodland habitats throughout Florida, except the Keys, and can reach 90 feet in height. Characterized by a broad crown and thick warty trunk, sugarberry soon becomes a dominant shade tree in areas where it is planted. Its large strong branches provide homes for many species of wildlife. Small greenish flowers are produced in the spring, followed by large crops of ¼-inch plum-colored fruit that ripen in early fall.

Although the fruit have a rather thin flesh, they are eaten by many songbirds and other wildlife. Sugarberry is a host for the caterpillars of numerous moths and a few butterflies; as such, it provides food for insectivorous birds and other wildlife. Because of its large size and very broad crown, sugarberry is best used as a shade tree. In landscapes of sufficient size, it can also be effectively used as an overstory component of a mixed-forest landscape. It has one significant drawback for use in a

Sugarberry (*Celtis laevigata*).
Photo by the author.

landscape: sugarberry will form root suckers and spread. Do not use this tree in areas where it might be difficult to confine. Young trees will also sprout from the large crops of bird-dispersed fruit. This is an adaptable tree for most landscape settings, but it is not salt tolerant.

Hawthorns

I confess that I think hawthorns (*Crataegus* spp.) are among the most useful and beautiful groups of native trees available for wildlife landscapes in north and central Florida. I shamelessly promote them whenever I speak at public meetings, but they remain largely unavailable from the commercial nursery trade. Hawthorns are small (generally 20 to 30 feet) deciduous trees in the rose family. Like the apples and plums (also in this family), they bloom profusely in the spring with bright white five-petal flowers. In some species, the flowers are produced in clusters along the young branches while in others the blooms are solitary and scattered. These attract a wide variety of pollinators. Hawthorns are monoecious and produce applelike fruit known as haws or hips that are a valued wildlife food. Ripe haws are rich in vitamin C and can be used to make jelly. Some are sold commercially in health food markets as well. Hawthorns are thorny, but the degree of thorniness varies both within and among species. Because of their thorniness and strong branches, they are excellent cover choices for many nesting birds and other wildlife. Hawthorns give plant taxonomists fits because even the recognized species vary greatly in characteristics such as leaf shape. Some taxonomists have described more than 700 species in North America, whereas others have condensed the total number to several dozen. I will describe the few species both obviously distinct and generally available, and I will use the taxonomy currently generally accepted, but taxonomic changes are sure to come, and as many as 46 species of hawthorns are being considered for Florida. Some of the biggest changes will come within the species currently known as "summer" haw (*C. flava*). All our native hawthorns make excellent choices for the wildlife landscape and should be used more often. Most grow rather quickly and produce fruit at about 7 years of age. None are tolerant of salts. As members of the rose family, hawthorns are especially attractive to browsing wildlife such as rabbits and white-tailed deer, and they are host plants for a variety of butterfly and moth caterpillars.

May Haw (*C. aestivalis*)

May haw is a 20-foot tree with a somewhat crooked, gray-barked trunk and irregular crown. The leaves are small, oval, and slightly toothed, although some leaves are lobed. May haw is generally armed with straight spines between ½ and ¾ inch in length. The white to pinkish white flowers occur singly or in groups of two or three. The ⅓-inch bright red fruit ripen in early summer, normally in May. These fruit are prized for jelly making, and a small commercial business has developed around them. May haw is native to wet- and moist-soil woodlands of north and north central Florida, but it is adaptable to average soils once established, and it can be grown throughout central Florida. Use it in filtered sun or in partly sunny locations. Because of its growth form, it is not the best haw for use as a specimen tree. Its best use is as part of an understory planting in a mixed-species woodland.

May haw (*Crataegus aestivalis*). Photo by the author.

Cockspur Haw/Wakulla Haw
(*C. crus-galli*, syn. *C. pyracanthoides*)

Cockspur haw is rarely available, but it has many traits that recommend it to a wildlife landscape. I have included it here in hope that some demand might arise for it and that it will eventually become more widely grown. Cockspur haw is armed with stout straight spines that may be 1½ inches in length. At maturity, it is a 25-foot tree with dark, scaly bark and a rather rounded crown with widely spreading branches. The small oval leaves are only slightly toothed along the margins and quite shiny and deep green in color. White to pinkish flowers occur in numerous clusters in the spring.

The small fruit, about ⅓ inch in diameter, ripen by summer. Their color ranges from dull red to rusty orange or greenish, and they frequently are mottled with blackish spots. This adaptable hawthorn is native mostly to upland sites in north and north central Florida, but it is adaptable and can be grown effectively well into central Florida. This is one hawthorn that makes an exceptional specimen tree.

Cockspur haw (*Crataegus crus-galli*).
Photo by the author.

Summer Haw/Yellow Haw (*C. flava,* syn. *C. floridana, C. lacrimata, C. michauxii, C. pulcherrima*)

Summer haw is one of the haws that has most confused plant taxonomists. Recent work has determined that the true summer haw (*C. flava*) does not even occur in Florida, and that the one sold here as "summer haw" is really a dozen or so closely related species. Currently, some of our most respected taxonomists have begun separating out one of the most common types as *C. michauxii*, but many more are likely to be recognized as separate species in the years ahead. For the purpose of this book, I have combined them under one name, using the Latin name most widely used at the present. Summer haw is a widely occurring and variable species, distributed in upland communities throughout north and central Florida. Generally a 15–20-foot tree with a very wide-spreading crown, it has an almost bonsai appearance with its short, crooked trunk and crown of crooked, sometimes weeping, branches. The toothed leaves are broad and spatula shaped; sometimes lobed. Thorniness is variable, with some specimens being nearly thornless. The thorns, when present, are stout and

Summer haw (*Crataegus flava*). Photo by the author.

¼–½ inch long. Large white flowers bloom singly or in small clusters in the spring. The large (½–¾-inch) globe-shaped fruit vary in color from greenish yellow to reddish and ripen by summer. Their relatively large size limits their use to larger birds and mammals. This hawthorn is adapted to well-drained sandy soils and prefers sunny locations. Use it as a specimen tree or in an open sunny landscape setting.

Parsley Haw (*C. marshallii*)

Parsley haw is a 20-foot slender tree native to moist and wet woodlands in north and central Florida. Often multitrunk, it has rather short crooked branches and a narrow crown. Because of this, it is not as good a wildlife cover plant as some other members of this genus. Thorns, when present, are slender and about ½ inch long. The leaves are small with many deeply notched lobes that resemble the leaves of curled parsley. Numerous clusters of small white to pinkish white flowers bloom in the spring. Clusters of narrow, bright red, ¼-inch fruit ripen by fall and persist into winter,

if they are not gobbled by birds and other wildlife. Parsley haw is a beautiful and delicate tree best used in a partly shady woodland understory. It is adaptable but may need extra water to get it established.

Parsley haw (*Crataegus marshalli*). Photo by the author.

Littlehip Haw (*C. spathulata*)

Littlehip haw is another hawthorn that deserves to be more widely planted. This is a 20-foot tree native to moist woodland habitats of north Florida. Like many others in this genus, however, it adapts well to average landscape settings and prospers well into central Florida. This haw shares some of the same characteristics as parsley haw, but its leaves are linear, unlobed to deeply lobed, but never sharply toothed. The trees are sometimes thornless. The thorns, when present, are stout, straight, and 1 to 1½ inches long. The trees are often multitrunk, and the outer bark on mature specimens peels away in thin plates, revealing an orange-brown inner bark. This adds

to the tree's aesthetic character. Numerous clusters of small white or pinkish white flowers in the spring develop into many bright red ¼-inch-long cylindrical fruit in the fall. These will persist into winter if not eaten first. Because these fruit are so small, they are easily available to even the smallest songbird. As with parsley haw, use this tree in the understory of a mixed woodland, but give it enough light to bloom and set fruit properly.

Littlehip haw (*Crataegus spathulata*). Photo by the author.

Green haw (*Crataegus viridis*). Photo by the author.

Green Haw (*C. viridis*)

Green haw is a slender 25-foot tree native to moist- and wet-soil habitats of north and central Florida. Although it prefers a bit of extra moisture, it will adapt to more typical landscape conditions once established. Green haw is often largely spineless; the spines, when present, are thin, and ½ to 1 inch long. Green haw is characterized by its wide-spreading branches and rounded crown. Leaves are rather large and triangular in shape, with several to many pointed lobes and a noticeably toothed margin, giving them the appearance somewhat of maple leaves. Small white flowers occur in numerous clusters during the spring. The ¼–⅓-inch rounded orange-red fruit ripen by fall. Green haw may be difficult to find commercially, but its attractive appearance and wildlife qualities make the search worthwhile.

Hickories

The hickories (*Carya* spp.) are a group of large deciduous trees characterized by featherlike compound leaves, dense heavy wood, and hard-shelled nuts. They are often a dominant component of the plant community in which they occur. The crowns and strong branches provide excellent cover for wildlife. The oil-rich nuts are a prized food source for mammals, particularly squirrels and other woodland rodents, but most species are not particularly tasty for human consumption. Nut crops are annually abundant once the trees mature, but they grow slowly. Some species don't produce nuts until they are many decades old, and even the quickest to mature take 15–20 years. Hickory foliage is not attractive to most browsing mammals. A large number of moth caterpillars, however, have adapted to use it, so it has some value to nestling and adult birds. Hickories are monoecious. Most are not especially salt tolerant.

Mockernut Hickory (*C. alba*, syn. *C. tomentosa*)

Mockernut hickory is a large (to 100 feet) hickory with a tall straight trunk and rounded crown. The undersides of the leaflets (normally seven per leaf) and the leaf stems are tomentose (i.e., fuzzy), hence the formerly accepted scientific name. The common name is derived from the difficulty experienced by early settlers trying to crack the thick shells of the nuts. The kernels are sweet, but difficult for most animals, except rodents, to eat. They are also large: between

Mockernut hickory (*Carya alba*). Photo by Shirley Denton, with permission.

1½ and 3 inches long. Mockernut hickory is native to fertile upland soils of north Florida and is not recommended for areas much south of this range.

Scrub Hickory (*C. floridana*)

Scrub hickory is a medium-sized (rarely taller than 30 feet) tree native to deep, well-drained, sandy soils in peninsular Florida. It can be used nearly statewide, given proper drainage. Unlike its larger cousins, scrub hickory has a short, straight trunk (or several trunks) and a rather crooked "bonsai" aspect. The twisting branches and wide-spreading crown give it character. Its leaves usually are composed of three or five leaflets, sometimes seven, and are yellowish green in color. The thick-shelled nuts, 1 to 1½ inches long, have sweet kernels excellent for human consumption. They also are eagerly sought by wildlife. This is an excellent hickory for sandy areas, including coastal dunes, as long as the tree is not inundated with saltwater.

Scrub hickory (*Carya floridana*). Photo by the author.

Pignut Hickory (*C. glabra*)

Pignut hickory is native to woodland habitats throughout most of Florida, except the extreme southern counties. This tree may reach more than 100 feet in height in fertile upland soil and live more than 250 years. Pignut hickory has a large straight trunk and broad rounded crown that provides good cover. Leaves usually have five or seven leaflets that are deep green. The 1–2-inch nuts have a relatively thick shell, but less so than scrub hickory. The sweetness of the kernels varies greatly. Pignut hickory has the best fall color among Florida species, turning bright yellow in late fall. It is also the species most widely available from nurseries.

Pignut hickory (*Carya glabra*). Photo by the author.

Sand Hickory (*C. pallida*)

Sand hickory is a 30–50-foot tree native to sandy upland soils in the western and central Panhandle. I have included it, even though it is rarely available from nurseries, because it is a beautiful member of the group and deserving of more attention. It is similar in appearance to pignut hickory, but the undersides of the leaves are much paler and the smaller nuts (1½ inches long) have a thinner shell. The kernels are sweet and eagerly sought by wildlife. This hickory has good wildlife value, but its limited range in

Sand hickory (*Carya pallida*). Photo by the author.

Florida likely reduces its potential use to the northern third of Florida; the extent of its planting range in Florida has not been well tested, however.

Hollies

Few families of native plants are more useful to wildlife than the hollies (*Ilex* spp.). This family is well represented in Florida by a variety of deciduous and evergreen trees and shrubs native to a wide diversity of habitats. Hollies are dioecious and should be planted in groupings, but some species will cross-pollinate others. Most produce fruit at an early age, and this food is extensively used by birds and small mammals. Most species also provide excellent cover because of their dense foliage and branching structure. The foliage is not extensively eaten by browsing wildlife such as rabbits and white-tailed deer or by the caterpillars of butterflies and moths. Hollies produce dependable and abundant crops of fruit each year, generally in the fall, and hold their fruit well into the winter months when most other foods have disappeared. For that reason, they are especially important to many migratory and resident songbirds. All hollies contain some amount of caffeine in their foliage, but only one, yaupon holly (*I. vomitoria*), has been widely used as a tea substitute. Some worthwhile species are not commercially available or have very limited ranges in Florida. The others are described below.

Carolina Holly (*I. ambigua*)

Carolina holly is a deciduous, shrubby tree that may reach about 15 feet in height, but is often only 6 to 10 feet tall. It is adaptable to a wide variety of growing conditions, from white sand scrubs to fertile woodlands, but requires good drainage. Do not plant this holly in sites where standing water is common or where salt tolerance is important. This is one of my favorite hollies because of its shiny rich green foliage and bright red ⅓-inch fruit. Fruit ripen in late summer and will persist well into winter after the leaves fall. During the winter, its leafless form, covered in deep red fruit,

is a beautiful sight. Carolina holly is native from north to south central Florida and can be used nearly throughout the state, except in the extreme southern peninsula. Because of its rather open habit, it is not a good source of nesting cover. Use this species as part of a mixed hedge or in the understory of a mixed-woodland planting. Carolina holly is not often commercially available and may be difficult to find. It is my hope that more demand for it by wildlife gardeners will encourage more nurseries to propagate it.

Carolina holly (*Ilex ambigua*).
Photo by the author.

Dahoon holly (*Ilex cassine*). Photo by the author.

Dahoon Holly (*I. cassine*)

Dahoon holly is an evergreen tree that may reach 25 feet in height. Although it occurs naturally as a common component of wetland forests, it is very adaptable to growing conditions and will even prosper in parking lot median strips and other hot, dry, sunny locations. It is Florida's most widely distributed holly, occurring throughout the state, including the Keys. As such, it is the one holly that will prosper in nearly any landscape setting statewide. Dahoon holly is an excellent wildlife plant and can be used in a wide variety of landscape settings—including areas that receive moderate salt spray. Its deep green leaves are without the spiny teeth common to the American holly, and its straight trunk and light-colored bark lend aesthetic qualities when used as a specimen tree or within a mixed-forest setting. The fruit are normally bright red (a yellow fruited form is available commercially) and small (1¼ inches in diameter), making them ideal for songbirds. Fruit crops are dependable each year and are held on the tree well into late winter, if they are not eaten first.

Possumhaw Holly (*I. decidua*)

Possumhaw holly is another deciduous holly that is, sadly, not often commercially available in Florida; however, it has many attributes in its favor and is worth seeking out. If you are determined to add this one, make sure you are getting Florida stock. Possumhaw holly is often offered by out-of-state sources, but these plants rarely perform well in Florida. This is a shrubby holly native to lowland woods in north and central Florida. It can be successfully grown nearly statewide, except in the extreme southern peninsula, but will perform best as a component of a mixed-woodland landscape where the soils are moist to wet. It is not salt tolerant. Possumhaw holly may eventually grow to a small tree about 30 feet tall, but it is unlikely to be more than a 10–15-foot shrub here in Florida. The ⅓-inch

fruit are orange red in color and persist well into winter. This holly is similar in appearance to the more widely used but evergreen yaupon holly, but it has received far less attention in Florida as a landscape plant.

Possumhaw holly (*Ilex decidua*). Photo by Shirley Denton, with permission.

Common Gallberry (*I. glabra*)

Common gallberry is a small (to 8 feet) evergreen shrub common in much of Florida's pine flatwoods habitats and wetland edges, except in extreme southern regions. It is widely grown by the native plant nursery trade but is most often used in pineland mitigation projects, not in home landscape plantings. In many respects, this is understandable. Gallberry is not the most attractive or useful native holly for wildlife landscapes, but it is extremely adaptable and can be added to a mixed hedge, for example, with good results. The shiny evergreen leaves and black fruit give it some landscape appeal, but the bitterness of the ⅓-inch fruit greatly reduces its food value. In most settings, gallberry is the last fruit remaining during the winter months after the birds arrive. While this can be a positive attribute in some settings, I have seen the fruit go unused and shrivel on the parent plant. Seemingly, wildlife consume these fruit only when nothing else is left. Its small stature and thin branches offer little cover value as well. Gallberry has relatively low tolerance of salt.

Gallberry (*Ilex glabra*). Photo by the author.

Tawnyberry Holly (*I. krugiana*)

Tawnyberry holly (*Ilex krugiana*). Photo by Shirley Denton, with permission.

Tawnyberry holly is restricted to south Florida and is the state's only cold-sensitive holly. Although this greatly restricts its use in Florida, its attributes make it a good choice for the wildlife landscape in those regions that rarely see frost. Tawnyberry holly is best used as an understory shrub in a south Florida hammock landscape with limestone soils. It is an evergreen shrub that can eventually reach 30 feet in height. Its leaves are broad with long pointed tips, somewhat resembling the leaves of some cherries. Tawnyberry holly produces dependable annual crops of black ¼-inch fruit that ripen in late summer. Prior to fully ripening, they are yellowish red—hence the common name. The thin drooping branches of tawnyberry holly provide little nest support for songbirds, but its evergreen nature provides hiding cover, especially when planted in clusters within a mixed-understory planting. Tawnyberry holly has very good salt and drought tolerance and can be planted in a variety of soils, including those that are highly alkaline.

Myrtle Holly/Myrtle Dahoon Holly
(*I. myrtifolia*, syn. *I. cassine* var. *myrtifolia*)

Myrtle holly is one of three hollies I have included that are often difficult to find commercially. Why this species seems largely ignored by Florida growers and landscapers is a mystery to me, but perhaps some attention from all of us will help to rectify this. Myrtle holly, sometimes referred to as myrtle dahoon, is closely related to the dahoon holly, described above. Some plant experts consider it merely a distinct variety. Unlike the dahoon holly, it is most often a many-branched shrub and not a single-trunk tree. Under the best conditions, myrtle holly can grow to 25 feet, but it is often much shorter. Myrtle holly is native to the northern two-thirds of Florida; it is most abundant in wetland areas though adaptable to a wider range of growing conditions. A distinctive feature of this holly is its small, narrow, evergreen leaves. This and its open character reduce its value as a cover plant, but its ¼-inch, orange-red fruit (a yellow-fruited form is sometimes available) are used by many wildlife. Use myrtle holly in a mixed hedge or as an accent shrub where its foliage and fruit can be better admired. Its tolerance of salt is poorly reported but likely similar to that of the dahoon.

Myrtle holly (*Ilex myrtifolia*).
Photo by the author.

American Holly (*I. opaca*)

American holly and its various cultivars and hybrids (e.g., East Palatka and Savannah holly) are some of the most commonly planted native trees in North America. Its relatively slow growth is balanced by its adaptability and long life. American holly is native to the northern two-thirds of Florida in a variety of soil conditions and can be used effectively nearly statewide in a wide variety of settings. It tolerates moderate salt and, if used as a component of a mixed-forest planting, a great deal of shade. Its structure and fruit production are substantially enhanced, however, by moderate sunlight and good soil fertility. American holly may eventually reach 45 feet in height but in most settings will rarely exceed 30 feet. American holly can be effectively incorporated into a wide variety of native plant landscapes. As a specimen tree, its evergreen foliage and straight light-barked trunk are aesthetically interesting. In a mixed woodland, its narrow crown makes room for other species, and its spiny leaves enhance the cover value of everything surrounding it. Some forms lack the leaf spines typical for this species; do not select these varieties for most settings where wildlife cover is important. American holly also is a great source of food for many wildlife. The ⅓–½-inch fruit are normally bright red, a small size that makes them ideal for nearly every fruit-eating species of wildlife. Yellow-fruited forms are also available.

American holly (*Ilex opaca*). Photo by the author.

Yaupon holly (*Ilex vomitoria*). Photo by the author.

Yaupon Holly (*I. vomitoria*)

Yaupon holly is one of the most adaptable of all of Florida's native hollies and one of our best wildlife plants. Thankfully, it is also widely commercially available. This multitrunk shrub will eventually reach 25–30 feet in height and then become treelike. Many growth forms of this species are available, including dwarf cultivars ("Nana" and "Schilling's") and weeping ones ("Folsom's"). Yaupon holly is native to a wide variety of habitats throughout much of Florida, except the extreme southern peninsula. It has exceptional salt tolerance and will grow in nearly any soil and light condition. It may be best used, however, to create a thicket of wildlife hiding cover and/or as a major component of a mixed hedge. Its dense branching pattern and dark evergreen leaves provide excellent cover for songbirds and other wildlife. A well-grown specimen or cluster will provide ideal nesting conditions for such birds as cardinals and Carolina wrens. It also responds well to shearing if your tastes or landscape setting require a more managed appearance. Yaupon is an excellent food producer. The dependable crops of ¼-inch, shiny red fruit serve as an important food source for a wide variety of songbirds and a few small mammals. The leaves make an excellent tea, despite its scientific name.

Locustberries

Locustberries are members of the malpighias, a moderate-sized family of trees, shrubs, and vines native to tropical regions of the world. The flowers and fruit of many species are often showy, and some are cultivated as ornamentals in greenhouses or warm climates. The non-native Barbadoscherry (*Malpighia glabra*) is commonly grown in south Florida for its red fleshy fruit. Malpighias are characterized by simple evergreen leaves and flowers in racemes with hooded clawed petals. All plants in this family are monoecious and have moderate salt tolerance.

Locustberry (*Byrsonima lucida*)

Locustberry is a broad-crowned, irregular shrub (to about 15 feet) native to the pine rockland forests of the Keys. It can be grown throughout south Florida in locations that do not freeze. Its short, thin branches can be identified by the prominent joints on the twigs; they do not offer much for wildlife cover. Locustberry's value to wildlife is primarily as a food source. Numerous white or pink flowers are produced mostly in the spring. The blooms typically change color to yellow or rose red after several days, and

Locustberry (*Brysonima lucida*). Photo by the author.

they attract a wide variety of insect pollinators. Numerous ¼-inch fruit, similar to tiny peaches, ripen to red by summer and are eagerly consumed by birds and other wildlife. Locustberry is an attractive landscape addition, but its use is restricted to areas of Florida where cold temperatures are not normally encountered. Birds are not likely to nest in its spindly branches, but its dense foliage provides good concealment once the plant is mature. This plant is best used in small clusters and combined with other shrubs and small trees as part of a mixed planting. Flowering and fruiting will be best if it is not shaded too much.

Magnolias

Magnolias (*Magnolia* spp.) in Florida are small to large trees with large leaves, relatively straight trunks, and rather crooked branches. Many of our species have very restricted ranges in north Florida and prefer moist fertile soils. The others are very widely distributed and commonly used in landscapes. Magnolias produce showy white flowers in the spring, and these develop into fruiting cones containing numerous seeds, covered by red flesh, eaten by birds and other wildlife after they ripen in the fall. All our species are monoecious. Magnolias have only moderate wildlife value, although they frequently are planted for their beauty. The other member of this family, the tulip tree (*Liriodendron tulipifera*), has less wildlife value and is not discussed here.

Southern Magnolia (*M. grandiflora*)

Southern magnolia is one of the grandest symbols of southern landscapes. This evergreen magnolia often reaches 65 feet in height and has a distinct pyramidal shape. The large leathery leaves enhance its cover value for wildlife, and its adaptability to a range of growing conditions allows its use in a variety of settings, including coastal areas. Although its natural range extends only to south central Florida, it is grown in cultivation even in southern areas of the state. The large fragrant flowers produce good fruit crops annually. Because of its spreading shape, southern magnolia is best planted as a specimen tree. If planted as part of a mixed hammock, make sure to establish the other trees early to make sure they have room and

Southern magnolia (*Magnolia grandiflora*). Photo by the author.

force the magnolia to grow upward instead of outward. Even then, give this tree some room between other members of your planting.

Sweetbay (*M. virginiana*)

Sweetbay is the only other native magnolia widely available from commercial sources in Florida. Although it is not planted as commonly as the southern magnolia, it has the widest natural distribution of any of our native magnolias and occurs naturally throughout the state, except the Keys, in moist-soil habitats. It is quite adaptable and thrives in most growing conditions except where exposed to salt. Sweetbay is an attractive tree, 60 to 70 feet tall, with medium-sized, elliptical evergreen leaves; smooth whitish bark; and a narrow crown. Its narrowness diminishes its value as wildlife cover, but songbirds manage to hide in its evergreen foliage. The undersides of the leaves are silvery pubescent, adding to its beauty whenever a breeze blows. Leaves have a distinctive fragrance when crushed and may be used in cooking. They also are the larval food source for eastern tiger swallowtail butterflies. One drawback to the use of this tree is its

Sweetbay magnolia (*Magnolia virginiana*). Photo by the author.

tendency to produce roots at the soil surface that can sucker if disturbed by such activities as mowing or planting.

Maples

Maples are common throughout North America and are most often trees, sometimes shrubs. All five species of maples native to Florida are deciduous trees. Maples are useful shade trees and commonly planted in developed landscapes because they grow quickly, are relatively pest free and very adaptable to growing conditions, and have good form, but they are not especially important to wildlife. The winged seeds, always produced in the spring, are eaten mostly by squirrels and other rodents. The foliage is a preferred food of white-tailed deer, when they can reach it. Maples produce very little food for songbirds, however. Their "tight" bark does not provide especially good cover for insects, but their foliage is consumed by a great many species of caterpillars, and these can be an important food source for some insectivorous birds. The crowns provide cover for nesting birds and other wildlife. Although maples generally grow rather quickly to maturity, most species are weak and relatively short lived. Two maples are well suited to Florida landscapes; neither is salt tolerant.

Red Maple (*Acer rubrum*)

Red maple is the most wide ranging and commonly used maple in Florida. At maturity, red maples may reach 90 feet in height, although they rarely exceed 60 feet in Florida. They occur principally in hardwood wetlands throughout the state, but will grow well in soils of nearly any condition except those of extremely high pH or excessive drainage. Red maples get their name from the color of their flowers and newly developing seeds in early spring and the color of their leaves in fall. Most trees are dioecious, with the males producing none of the distinctive winged seeds, but some have bisexual flowers and are monoecious. Red maple leaves are extremely variable in shape and can confuse identification. Florida trees do not need cold temperatures to produce flowers and fruit, but out-of-state stock do and should be avoided, especially in central and south Florida. Red maples often begin producing seeds when they are 4–5 years old and are one of the first trees in spring to flower and bear fruit. Good seed crops occur nearly every year on mature specimens.

Red maple (*Acer rubrum*). Photo by the author.

Florida Sugar Maple
(*A. saccharum* subsp. *floridanum*; syn *A. barbatum*)

Florida sugar maple is a distinct subspecies of common sugar maple, which ranges across eastern North America. It generally is smaller than northern sugar maples (about 30–40 feet at maturity) with smaller three- or five-lobed leaves and whitish bark. The leaves turn bright yellow or muted orange in fall in north and north central Florida, turning brown by winter. Specimens planted farther south may not get any fall color, however. Unlike those of other maples, the brown leaves tend to remain on the tree until spring. Florida sugar maple occurs naturally in moist upland sites (often in alkaline soils) in north and central Florida. It can be successfully grown throughout this region, given soils that are not excessively drained. This is the strongest and most long-lived native maple species and works especially well as a component of a mixed-forest landscape.

Florida sugar maple (*Acer saccharum* subsp. *floridanum*). Photo by the author.

Marlberry and Myrsine

The large family of plants that includes these widely used native shrubs is mostly tropical. The two native species occur naturally in much of peninsular Florida. Both have broad oval evergreen leaves and small round purple fruit eaten mostly by birds and small mammals.

Marlberry (*Ardisia escallonioides*)

Marlberry is a common understory shrub of hammock habitats from coastal central Florida counties through much of south Florida. In central Florida, where it might be damaged by freezing temperatures, it often does not exceed 4 feet in height. In south Florida, it may reach 20 feet. Given the right conditions, marlberry is one of the best landscaping choices for

shady areas. The richly aromatic, white flowers bloom profusely at the crowns of each of the branches and create a beautiful sight. They also attract a wide variety of insect pollinators. Flowers occur at various times of year, and these are followed several months later by purple, ⅓-inch marblelike fruit. Marlberry is monoecious. Individual marlberry shrubs do not provide much cover value. Although the broad evergreen leaves create a visual screen, individual plants have relatively weak branches that are widely

Marlberry (*Ardisia escallonioides*). Photo by the author.

spaced on the trunk. For these reasons, marlberry is best used in clusters and/or as part of a mixed understory planted as a thicket. In this way, its attributes are best accented and it creates good hiding cover for songbirds and other wildlife.

Myrsine (*Rapanea punctata*; syn. *Myrsine floridana, M. guianensis, R. guianensis*)

Myrsine is a single-trunk, shrubby tree native to coastal and inland hammock habitats from north central to southern Florida. It has more tolerance of cold than marlberry and can be used along the coast of Florida where the temperature does not get much below the mid-20s Fahrenheit. Myrsine may reach 20 feet in height. Unlike its cousin described above, myrsine is dioecious, and the flowers are inconspicuous and nonfragrant. They also appear along the sides of the branches in late winter. Round, ¼-inch blackish fruit ripen on the female plants in late summer and are used by some songbirds and small mammals. Myrsine will sucker and form thickets if allowed. As a thicket, it provides good cover, but the short, thin branches do not encourage bird nesting.

Myrsine (*Rapanea punctata*). Photo by the author.

Mulberries

Mulberries are in the same family as figs. Both produce abundant crops of sweet succulent fruit eagerly sought by wildlife and dispersed by birds. Because of this, they tend to rapidly colonize disturbed openings in woodland habitats. They are also fast-growing but relatively short-lived trees that mature quickly. Of the mulberries, only the red mulberry is native.

Red Mulberry (*Morus rubra*)

Red mulberry is a 40-foot deciduous tree native to most of Florida except the extreme south. As such, it can be planted nearly statewide in areas not subjected to salts. Red mulberry is a common midcanopy tree of forested habitats. It will thrive in these conditions, but fruit production is greatly enhanced when it is grown in at least partial sun. The broad, spreading crown and numerous branches give it good cover value. Red mulberry is dioecious. Flowering occurs in the spring, and fruit ripen on the female trees about two months later. The cylindrical 1-inch-long juicy purple fruit are prized by birds and mammals, but the purple stains caused by their droppings can be a nuisance. Although best known for its fruit, mulberry

Red mulberry (*Morus rubra*). Photo by Shirley Denton, with permission.

may be most important to wildlife because of the significant numbers of small pollinating insects it attracts with its blooms during the spring. If you are a serious birdwatcher, you know there is no better place to see warblers and other songbirds during migration than in the crown of a blooming mature red mulberry. The diversity of birds it attracts is absolutely amazing. Although mulberries are excellent plants for wildlife, their spreading growth habit and the staining potential of their fruit should be considered prior to planting so your neighbors won't be offended. If staining is a concern, consider planting a male instead of a female.

Oaks

This family is well represented in Florida and contains many well-known species commonly used in urban landscapes. Besides the 23 species of oaks native to Florida, the family includes beeches and chestnuts. The American beech is described above, but the American chestnut (*Castanea dentata*) has been virtually eliminated by chestnut blight disease. It is not included in this text, although it was once an exceedingly important component of the eastern deciduous forest. All members of this family are monoecious.

True oaks produce calorie-rich nuts important in the diet of many species of wildlife, but especially of mammals such as squirrels and other rodents, raccoons, opossums, and white-tailed deer. Birds such as jays, woodpeckers, bobwhite quail, and wild turkey also use the nuts of some species. Many oaks do not produce dependable crops each year, but follow a good year with several years of almost no production. Acorn size is variable among species. Although mammals are able to eat acorns of any size, small birds such as bobwhite quail are unable to eat those that are too large. Oaks are generally divided into two main groups: white and red. As a very general rule, white oaks have leaves with rounded lobes, while red oaks have leaves with pointed ones—but because some oaks have leaves without lobes, this trait is not always obvious. White oak acorns mature in the fall of their first year, while red oak acorns do not mature until their second fall. Trees in the white oak group tend to produce fairly large, heavy acorns, whereas those in the red oak group tend to have smaller ones. Acorns from trees in the red oak group are typically higher in protein, fat, and calories than acorns from trees in the white oak group. These are favorable characteristics for wildlife consumption, but red oak acorns also tend to be higher in fiber and tannins, which reduces their digestibility and makes them somewhat less desirable. Ultimately, acorns produced by trees in the white oak group tend to be consumed more regularly by wildlife than those from the red oak group. Species found in Florida with exceptionally high protein acorns include southern red (*Q. falcata*), shumard (*Q. shumardii*), and post oak (*Q. stellata*); those with particularly high fat content come from bluejack (*Q. incana*), southern red, and water oak (*Q. nigra*). Acorns from trees in the white oak group germinate shortly after falling from the tree. This means the acorns are available for only a short period of time to terrestrial wildlife. In contrast, acorns from trees in the red oak group enter a period of dormancy after falling from trees and are available for longer periods of time.

Oaks generally grow rather quickly, but do not mature enough to produce acorns until they are 10–15 years old. In addition to producing acorns, oaks are significant for insect-eating songbirds. Many dozens of moth and butterfly species in Florida use oaks as their larval food plant, and these caterpillars provide an important food source for nestling and adult songbirds. The tiny flowers of oaks are a magnet for small pollinating insects during the spring, and the twigs and bark provide a haven for small beetles and other insects during the rest of the year. These insects, in turn, draw in migratory and resident songbirds in huge numbers. Finally, the foliage of young oaks is an important food for browsing mammals such as white-tailed deer and rabbits. Oaks are a varied group of woody plants that include trees and shrubs, and this influences their value as wildlife cover. Identification of individual oaks is sometimes difficult because leaf shape can differ greatly, even on the same tree. Hybridization between species can also occur. Some species have salt tolerance, and I mention those specifically in the descriptions below. None are cold sensitive. Most oaks are best used as specimen trees or as the dominant trees of a forested hammock. Few species are very tolerant of shade, so they should be planted in sunny locations or in sunny patches within an established woodland.

To help the reader, I have organized the oaks into two groups (white and red) and arranged each group alphabetically by Latin name. I have not included species that are not often available commercially, but these species also have good wildlife value. Oaks, in particular, play a dominant role in the flora of many of Florida's natural communities. Urban landscapes, however, often fail to take advantage of the great diversity of this family and rely too frequently on a handful of species.

White Oaks

White Oak (*Quercus alba*)

White oak occurs in Florida only in the northern Panhandle, in moist fertile soils. It is not well adapted to landscapes outside of north Florida and is best planted in soils of moderate moisture and fertility. This straight-trunk deciduous tree has a broad rounded crown and may reach 100 feet in height. The distinctive lobed leaves turn wine red in fall and brown in winter. The brown leaves often are held on the tree until spring. The acorns are ½ to ¾ inches long, and large crops are produced every four to six years.

White oak (*Quercus alba*). Photo by Shirley Denton, with permission.

Bluff Oak (*Q. austrina*)

Bluff oak may reach 100 feet at maturity and has an irregular and narrow crown. It occurs throughout north Florida; most often in well-drained woodland soils. Leaves are lobed somewhat like those of white oak, but their shape varies greatly within a tree. The lobes also tend to "droop." The acorns are ½ to ¾ inches long. Large crops are produced every four to six years.

Chapman Oak (*Q. chapmanii*)

Chapman oak is a small (to about 30 feet) deciduous tree common to well-drained sandy-soil areas throughout Florida, except the Keys. The slightly lobed to oval leaves are absent for only a brief period during the winter. It has a broad-spreading crown and irregular branches. The acorns

Left: Bluff oak (*Quercus austrina*). Photo by the author.

Above: Chapman oak (*Quercus chapmanii*). Photo by the author.

are quite broad and ¾ to 1 inch long. Good crops are produced every two to three years. This small oak has good tolerance of salt spray, and its relatively small size makes it adaptable to a wide variety of landscape settings. Because of its interesting shape, Chapman oak makes a good specimen tree for small landscapes with well-drained soils.

Sand Live Oak (*Q. geminata*)

Sand live oak is found throughout Florida, except at the extreme tip of the peninsula and in the Keys. It is native to deep, well-drained, sandy soils, including coastal dunes. Its mature height rarely exceeds 40 feet and is often less than 30 feet. When grown as a specimen, it has the same picturesque growth form as live oak, but in miniature. If allowed to sucker, it will form thickets. Its small, evergreen, linear leaves curl under at the margins and are "hairy" beneath. Its small, stiff branches provide good structure for nesting birds. Acorns are linear, about 1 inch long, and large crops are produced annually. As with the Chapman oak, described above, this small tree's stature, adaptability, and salt tolerance make it a good choice for many landscape settings where soils are sandy and well drained.

Sand live oak (*Quercus geminata*). Photo by the author.

Overcup oak (*Quercus lyrata*). Photo by Shirley Denton, with permission.

Overcup Oak (*Q. lyrata*)

Overcup oak is a 90-foot deciduous tree native to bottomland forest habitats west of the Suwannee River and the area around the Apalachicola River. It is adaptable to most landscape settings but best used in the Panhandle and the northern peninsula. Overcup oak has a tall straight trunk and broad rounded crown. Leaves are similar in shape to those of white oak, but longer and more linear. The acorns are round and slightly flattened, and between ¾ and 1 inch long. They are nearly completely enclosed by the cup; hence the tree's common name. Good acorn crops occur only every three or four years. Overcup oak is slow growing, but long lived. It makes a beautiful specimen tree when used in the right location.

Swamp Chestnut Oak (*Q. michauxii*)

Swamp chestnut oak is a large (to 100 feet) deciduous tree that occurs mostly in moist fertile soils in north and north central Florida. I have used this species as far south as Pinellas County, however, and it is very adaptable if given soils that are not excessively droughty. Its crown is relatively narrow, but its height and enormous, oval, many-lobed leaves help it get noticed. The leaves turn wine red in the fall. The acorns generally are 1–1½ inches long, and large crops occur sporadically, usually every four

Swamp chestnut oak
(*Quercus michauxii*).
Photo by the author.

to five years. This tree does well on alkaline soil and will tolerate flooding for brief periods.

Dwarf Live Oak (*Q. minima*)

Dwarf live oak is an evergreen, 3-foot shrub that forms extensive colonies by underground runners. Because of this, it acts more like a ground cover than a shrub. The leaves are stiff, leathery, and extremely variable in shape.

Dwarf live oak (*Quercus minima*). Photo by the author.

Most are long and linear, but others have poorly defined lobes and may be spiny. This oak occurs mostly in open sandy pinelands from north to south central Florida. It is tolerant of salt spray. Acorns are narrow and rather large, between ¾ and 1 inch long. Good crops generally occur every two to three years. Given a sunny, well-drained location, this oak can make an excellent cover thicket for wildlife, and its low-growing acorns are easily accessible before they fall to the ground.

Post Oak (*Q. stellata*)

Post oak is a medium-sized (about 60 feet) deciduous tree native to sandy soils in north and north central Florida. It can be grown in open, sunny locations well into south central Florida. One of the most distinctive features of this tree is its glossy green leaves, shaped somewhat like a crucifix. Post oaks are stout, short-limbed trees with rounded crowns. They also are slow growing, but long lived. Acorns are 1–1½ inches long, and good crops are produced every two to four years. This tree does not provide much for fall color, but its beautiful shape makes it an excellent specimen tree. A similar and closely related oak, the sand post oak (*Quercus margaretta*), is rarely offered and is not described here.

Post oak (*Quercus stellata*). Photo by the author.

Live Oak (*Q. virginiana*)

Live oak is the symbol of the southern landscape and requires little added description. Because of its broad crown, impressive size, and evergreen nature, this tree provides cover for many species of wildlife, and its large sprawling branches are used mostly by larger birds (i.e., owls and blue jays) and mammals for nesting. The outer branches, often draped in Spanish moss, provide nesting cover for orioles, painted buntings, and northern parula warblers. It is adaptable to a wide range of soil and water conditions, including salt, and its natural range extends statewide through the Florida Keys. Live oak is important as a food source because its 1-inch-long acorns are produced in abundance nearly every year. Although sometimes criticized as being a slow grower, live oak grows rather quickly when young and is especially long lived. Live oaks dominate the area where they are planted and often make adding other species difficult once they are established. For this reason, add understory plantings while the tree is young, and plan for the extensive shade they will ultimately produce.

Live oak (*Quercus virginiana*). Photo by the author.

Red Oaks

Southern Red Oak/Spanish Oak (*Q. falcata*)

Southern red oak is a large (to about 90 feet) deciduous tree that occurs throughout north and north central Florida in well-drained upland sites. It is adaptable to average landscape settings and makes a wonderful shade tree. The leaves have sharply pointed lobes and turn a rich red in autumn. The long straight trunk supports a broad rounded crown. The rounded acorns are about ½ inch long and produced in dependable annual crops.

Southern red oak (*Quercus falcata*). Photo by Shirley Denton, with permission.

Bluejack Oak (*Q. incana*)

Bluejack oak is a medium-sized (to about 40 feet) deciduous tree with an irregular trunk and open crown. The linear, willow-shaped leaves are bluish green. In spring, the new growth is pinkish. Bluejack oak is a common component of dry, sandy, open woods throughout north and central Florida; often growing with longleaf pine (*Pinus palustris*) and turkey oak (*Q. laevis*). The rounded acorns are about ½ inch long, and production is fairly reliable each year. This oak is rather fast growing but short lived. It does not produce much fall color.

Left: Bluejack oak (*Quercus incana*).
Photo by Shirley Denton, with
permission.

Below: Turkey oak (*Quercus laevis*).
Photo by the author.

Turkey Oak (*Q. laevis*)

Turkey oak is a 40–50-foot deciduous tree common to well-drained, sandy soils throughout north and central Florida. Like the bluejack oak, it is fast growing but short lived and has an open, irregular shape. The yellow-green leaves, normally with three or five sharply pointed lobes, are shaped somewhat like the outline of a turkey's foot. The leaves turn dark red in late fall. The rounded acorns are about 1 inch long and produced abundantly only every two to three years.

Laurel Oak/Diamond Oak (*Q. laurifolia*)

Laurel oak is perhaps the most widely planted oak in urban developments in Florida. Native to moist forest soils throughout the state north of the Everglades, laurel oak is adaptable and fast growing. It is not long lived, however, and rarely survives longer than 100 years. This deciduous tree may reach 100 feet in height. Trunks are straight, and the crowns are broad and round. Leaves are linear and without much fall color. Acorns are rounded, about 1 inch long, and good crops are produced annually. Some taxonomists distinguish a separate species of laurel oak, *Q. hemisphaerica*, and refer to *Q. laurifolia* only as diamond oak. *Q. hemisphaerica* is an upland species with narrower leaves than *Q. laurifolia*. I have chosen to follow the taxonomy of those who lump the two as one variable species.

Myrtle Oak (*Q. myrtifolia*)

Myrtle oak is a round-crowned, evergreen, shrubby tree that rarely exceeds 30 feet in height. Native to deep sandy soils from north to south Florida, including coastal dunes, it frequently forms thickets from root suckering. Such areas provide dense cover for wildlife. Myrtle oak has small, rounded, glossy leaves that are leathery and stiff. The small (¼ to ½ inch long) round acorns are produced reliably each year. Myrtle oak is not an especially good choice as a specimen tree, but it makes a good addition to a mixed-woodland setting in sunny locations with well-drained soils.

Water Oak (*Q. nigra*)

Water oak is a common 60-foot deciduous tree in north and central Florida in a variety of moist-soil habitats. It is very adaptable, however, to most landscape settings and can be grown nearly statewide. A rapid-growing but generally short-lived tree, water oak has a tall straight trunk and a rounded crown. The leaves are rather small and often spatula shaped (sometimes lobed). The rounded acorns are variable in size, but normally ½ to ¾ inch long. Good production occurs every one to two years. Water oak is sometimes considered a rather "weedy" species, but I find it attractive in a landscape setting.

Top left: Laurel oak (*Quercus laurifolia*). Photo by the author.

Bottom left: Myrtle oak (*Quercus myrtifolia*). Photo by the author.

Above: Water oak (*Quercus nigra*). Photo by the author.

Shumard oak (*Quercus shumardii*). Photo by the author.

Shumard Oak (*Q. shumardii*)

Shumard oak is a large (about 70 feet) deciduous tree native to north Florida in moist woodland habitats. Despite this, I have seen it used as a street tree as far south as south central Florida, proving it is both tolerant and adaptable outside its natural growing range. Shumard oak is an aesthetically attractive species, with a tall straight trunk and broad rounded crown. The shiny dark green leaves have seven, nine, or eleven deeply cut and sharply pointed lobes, and they turn a rich red in late fall after the first frost. The acorns are rounded and between ½ and 1 inch long. Good crops are produced every two to four years.

Olives

The olive family includes many important trees and shrubs, including the true olive (*Olea europaea*) and the commonly used non-native ligustrums (*Ligustrum* spp.) and jasmines (*Jasminum* spp.). It also includes four native genera that are wonderful wildlife plants: the fringetrees, privets (*Forestiera* spp.), ashes, and wild olives (*Osmanthus* spp.). Only the wild olives are discussed below. The others are treated under separate headings elsewhere.

Wild Olive/Devilwood (*O. americanus*)

Wild olive is a small evergreen tree that rarely exceeds 20 feet in height. It occurs throughout much of Florida, except the extreme southern counties, and is very adaptable to a variety of upland settings. Although its best growth occurs in fertile woodland areas, it tolerates deep, infertile sands in coastal and interior sites. It has very good salt tolerance and will prosper in sunny locations as well as in the understory of fairly shady woodlands. Wild olive is dioecious. The extremely aromatic flowers in the spring attract a diversity of pollinating insects, and the ½-inch olivelike fruit ripen in the fall. These are not especially attractive to most songbirds but are consumed by larger birds and small mammals. The branches of wild olive are strong, but it has a relatively open character, reducing its value as nesting and hiding cover. Use this small tree at the outer edges of a mixed-woodland planting where its wonderful fragrance can be admired.

Wild olive (*Osmanthus americanus*). Photo by the author.

Palms

Palms are not woody plants but related to grasses; nevertheless, their growth form is treelike or shrublike. Palms are characterized by stiff evergreen fronds that provide excellent cover for many species of wildlife when they are clustered around the growing tip. Palms with fronds that droop away from the center provide far less cover value. Most palms are monoecious and produce large amounts of rounded fruit composed of a fleshy exterior surrounding a hard inner nut. These can be very important to songbirds if the fruit is small, but some palm fruit are too large to be eaten by anything other than mammals and the largest birds, such as crows and jays. Numerous clusters of small, white, aromatic flowers attract bees, butterflies, and many other pollinating insects. Most palms in Florida flower during the early summer, and their fruit are ripe several months later. They are generally slow growers and slow to mature. Many species are available as adult specimens. Purchasing an adult palm is more expensive, but it reduces the wait for it to produce fruit and cover. Most palms have very high salt tolerance, are long lived, and are tolerant of nearly every type of growing condition in the home landscape. Some are understory shrubs, but most prefer sunny locations to prosper. I have not included a few of the rarest native palms, restricted to extreme south Florida, because they are difficult to find commercially, but even those species can be excellent choices in the right location.

Paurotis Palm (*Acoelorrhaphe wrightii*)

Paurotis palm is a slender, 20–30-foot tree that grows as a multitrunk clump. This small palm suckers near its base, so it slowly expands over time with trunks of varying sizes. Paurotis palm is found naturally only in extreme south Florida, but it can withstand winter temperatures into the mid-20s Fahrenheit. As such, it can be used in landscapes well into south central Florida. It also is adaptable to a variety of

Paurotis palm (*Acoelorrhaphe wrightii*). Photo by the author.

growing conditions, except the most well-drained, droughty soils. The large fan-shaped leaves are clustered near the growing tips, and the leaf stems are armed with stout curved spines; because of this, a mature specimen allowed to grow as a clump provides very good wildlife cover. Flowering occurs in winter or early spring. Numerous ¼-inch black fruit ripen mostly in the fall and provide a food source for many species of wildlife.

Needle Palm (*Rhapidophyllum hystrix*)

Needle palm is an understory shrub that rarely exceeds 6 feet in height. Resident to the shady understory of moist woodlands in north and central Florida, this palm is adaptable and survives well even in sunny parking lot plantings. It is one of the most cold-tolerant palms in the world, occurring naturally as far north as South Carolina. The leaves are deeply dissected and fan shaped, and they are densely clustered around the short trunk. When the fronds die and slough off, they leave long, slender, very sharply pointed needles at the base of each stem; therefore, groupings of these palms can provide excellent low cover for wildlife. Unlike our other native palms, needle palms are dioecious. The ⅓-inch, reddish brown

Needle palm (*Rhaphidophyllum hystrix*). Photo by the author.

fruit, which ripen in the fall, are used by some wildlife. The major wildlife value of this palm, however, comes from the dense cover it provides. This palm is best used in moist forest plantings to provide an evergreen accent, but make sure to put it away from walk areas, or its needles might cause problems.

Florida Royal Palm (*Roystonea elata*)

Florida royal palm is naturally a very rare plant in Florida, but it is widely used in our landscapes throughout the southern third of the peninsula because of its beauty. With its tall (to 130 feet), columnar, light gray trunk, its bright green shaft near the crown, and its large (to 13 feet), dark green, featherlike leaves, this palm is visually stunning. It is not one of the best palms, however, for wildlife. Because the long stiff fronds fall away from

Royal palm (*Roystonea regia*). Photo by the author.   Dwarf palm (*Sabal minor*). Photo by the autho

the crown in a rather loose arrangement, they provide little wildlife cover. Fruit production is seasonal, and the ½-inch bluish black berries ripen in the summer. Their large size limits their use to mammals and larger birds. For the wildlife landscape, royal palm is best used as a canopy tree within a mixed-forest planting.

Dwarf/Bluestem Palmetto (*Sabal minor*)

Dwarf palmetto is essentially a trunkless cabbage palm that rarely exceeds 6 feet in height. Like the needle palm, described above, it occurs mostly in the shady understory of moist woodlands. It has a wider distribution in Florida, however, and can be grown well into south Florida. The fan-shaped leaves are bluish green and without spines or teeth on the stem. When planted in masses in shady locations, dwarf palmetto can be both attractive and a valuable wildlife cover plant. The very fragrant white flowers of summer are followed by numerous ⅓-inch black fruit that ripen in late fall and are useful to many wildlife.

Cabbage Palm/Sabal Palm (*Sabal palmetto*)

Cabbage palm is Florida's state tree and occurs throughout the state in coastal and inland sites. Its best growth occurs in moist, fertile hammock soils, but it is extremely adaptable. The cabbage palm also is one of the best palms for wildlife. Often 60–80 feet tall, the dense rounded crown of fan-shaped leaves provides excellent hiding and nesting cover. Fragrant white flowers are produced in early summer, and numerous ⅓-inch black fruit ripen in the fall. Cabbage palm fruit are widely used by many songbirds and other wildlife.

Cabbage palm (*Sabal palmetto*). Photo by the author.

Saw Palmetto (*Serenoa repens*)

Saw palmetto is ubiquitous throughout Florida. It occurs nearly everywhere and grows in nearly every conceivable soil, water, and light condition. Because it is so common naturally, we have not fully valued this hardy and attractive plant in the landscape. Often nearly trunkless and 4–6 feet tall, it will sometimes develop noticeable trunks (especially in very wet soils) and grow to 20 feet in height. The dense leaves with small sawlike teeth along the stem produce excellent cover for wildlife. Fleshy, ¾-inch black fruit ripen in the late summer and are used mostly by mammals. An extract from this fruit is sometimes used as a herbal supplement to reduce the risk of prostate problems in men. Saw palmetto is best used as an understory cluster in open plantings where it will get at least a half-day of sun. Unlike other palms, it will form a new growing point from the trunk if severely pruned back. Do not use this plant in areas of high foot traffic as the teeth on the leaf stems can cause cuts. In areas where privacy is desired, however, or as a thicket to produce dense wildlife cover, this palm is an excellent choice. A distinct form with silvery blue leaves occurs along Florida's east coast and is often available commercially.

Saw palmetto (*Serenoa repens*). Photo by the author.

Florida Thatch Palm (*Thrinax radiata*)

Florida thatch palm is a small (15–20 feet) single-trunk palm native only to extreme south Florida. Although it is sometimes grown in landscapes outside its native range, it does not seem to have much tolerance for below-freezing temperatures. In the right location, this is a beautiful and useful addition to the wildlife landscape. Florida thatch palm (and its close cousin, the brittle or Key thatch palm, *T. morrisii*), prefers moist and relatively fertile soils, but is adaptable to most landscape settings except regular saltwater inundation. Its leaves, produced in a rounded clump near the crown, provide wildlife cover value. White fragrant flowers can be produced year-round but are most com-

Florida thatch palm (*Thrinax radiata*).
Photo by the author.

mon in the spring. These are followed several months later by ⅓-inch white fruit eagerly consumed by songbirds and other wildlife. Use this small palm as an accent tree, or scatter several in an open pineland landscape where they will get at least a half-day of sun.

Paradise Tree

Paradise tree (*Simarouba glauca*) is a member of the bitterbark family and a rather common inhabitant of well-drained hammocks in south Florida. It has some cold tolerance, and natural populations occur as far north as Cape Canaveral on the east coast. This is a slender, open-crowned

Paradise tree (*Simarouba glauca*). Photo by Shirley Denton, with permission.

evergreen tree with reddish brown and gray bark that may reach 50 feet in height. It is a rather slow grower and takes many years to produce flowers and fruit. Paradise tree has many aesthetic qualities that make it an attractive choice for a wildlife landscape. Its compound leaves are a rich orange- or purple-red when young and turn glossy green when fully formed. The dense foliage provides good hiding cover, but the slender branches are not conducive to nesting cover. Paradise tree is dioecious. Terminal clusters of light yellow flowers bloom mostly in early spring, and the reddish ¾-inch fruit ripen a few months later on the female trees. Fully ripe fruit are black. They are sweet and eagerly sought by birds and other wildlife. This tree has some tolerance of salts and should be grown in sunny upland locations in areas of the state where temperatures do not regularly fall below the mid-20s Fahrenheit. Although paradise tree makes an interesting accent tree, it is best used in a wildlife landscape as part of a mixed open-woodland planting. Because it is dioecious, it should be planted in small groupings.

Pawpaws

This family of trees and shrubs is well represented throughout Florida in a wide variety of habitats. All produce fleshy edible fruit readily eaten by small to medium-sized mammals, including rodents, opossums, raccoons, and foxes, but of little use to birds. Some also have fruit of limited use to people, but fruit production is often sporadic and not dependable because of their complex pollination strategy. Pawpaws are monoecious. The foliage is the larval food for the zebra swallowtail butterfly, and many butterfly gardeners look to add one of these species because of that. Most members of this family provide little value as wildlife cover. Most species are very difficult to find commercially, slow to mature, and difficult to establish in the landscape. One species, however, is a good exception and can be recommended for Florida landscapes.

Common Pawpaw/Dog Banana (*Asimina triloba*)

Common pawpaw is an attractive small deciduous tree (to about 30 feet) with large green leaves and small maroon flowers that produce a rather unpleasant odor. The leaves turn a brilliant yellow in the fall, however, adding an aesthetic quality to its use in the home landscape. Common pawpaw flowers in May or June, and its 2–3-inch fruit ripen several months later. Unlike other pawpaws in Florida, these fruit are rather tasty, and a small commercial market exists for them. Fruit production is variable and not especially reliable annually. This tree is native to the Florida Panhandle and not a good choice for areas farther south. It is shade tolerant and prefers rich, moist soils. It has only moderate salt tolerance. At best, it should be used in a mixed-forest setting and more for interest than for the amount of wildlife value it provides.

Common pawpaw (*Asimina triloba*). Photo by the author.

Persimmons

Persimmons are members of the mostly tropical ebony family. In Florida, the family is represented by only one species, described below.

Persimmon (*Diospyros virginiana*)

Persimmon is a 40–60-foot deciduous tree that occurs naturally throughout Florida except the Keys. It is extremely adaptable to a wide variety of growing conditions, has good salt tolerance, and offers good fall color in the northern half of the state. Persimmon can be found as an understory tree growing in shade and in open fields in full sun. In the home landscape, persimmon can be difficult to contain as it rapidly spreads by root suckers. Because of this, it is best suited to areas where it can be controlled or to a naturalized area where its spreading can be controlled by the presence of other species. Persimmons are dioecious, so only the females produce the 2-inch, yellow-orange fruit familiar to most of us. Wild persimmons are not as sweet as commercial varieties, but their fruit are especially prized by medium-sized mammals such as opossums and raccoons. They are too large for birds. Persimmons grown in sunny areas have some value as

Persimmon (*Diospyros virginiana*). Photo by Shirley Denton, with permission.

nesting and hiding cover. Trees grown in shady locations are often thin and too open to provide much cover value.

Pigeon Plum and Seagrape

These two medium-sized trees are members of the buckwheat family, a large family that includes many species of herbaceous weeds but only two species of native trees, in the genus *Coccoloba*. Both species are subtropical and restricted in nature to south central and south Florida. They have some tolerance to frost and can be grown in regions of central Florida where winter temperatures do not get below the upper 20s Fahrenheit. Their large, rounded, evergreen leaves provide good cover, and their racemes of late-spring/summer flowers attract many pollinating insects. Both species produce grapelike fruit on long clusters that ripen by fall; these are edible by humans and used by many species of wildlife. Both species are dioecious, have a strong tolerance of salt, and are adaptable to a wide variety of soil, moisture, and light conditions.

Pigeon Plum (*C. diversifolia*)

Pigeon plum is a medium-sized (30-foot) tree with a stout, straight trunk and a rounded, wide-spreading crown. It often produces multiple trunks nearly parallel to each other. Its dense, thick branches provide excellent nesting cover for birds. Flowering occurs in the spring, and the ⅓-inch purple fruit ripen by early fall. These are juicy and acidic and sometimes used to make jelly or wine. They are especially attractive to the threatened white-

Pigeon plum (*Coccoloba diversifolia*). Photo by the author.

crowned pigeons of extreme south Florida (hence, the tree's name), as well as to many other medium-sized to large birds and small mammals. Pigeon plum is native to upland coastal hammocks of south Florida. Although the tree is essentially evergreen, a leaf drop occurs in late spring, immediately followed by bright red regrowth. Pigeon plum has great ornamental and wildlife value and should be planted more than it currently is.

Seagrape (*C. uvifera*)

Seagrape is widely planted in landscapes throughout south and coastal central Florida. It is a shrubby tree that can reach 25 feet in areas without frost but is frequently shorter than that. Regardless of its ultimate size,

seagrape has a rather short main trunk and gnarled, irregular branches. It is exceptionally salt tolerant and a common component of coastal dunes from south central Florida southward. Seagrapes have large rounded leaves, shed irregularly during the year. The new growth is reddish, adding to the tree's overall aesthetic qualities in the landscape. Planted in a group, seagrapes provide valuable wildlife cover to birds and other wildlife, especially in coastal areas where such habitat is often difficult to provide. The large racemes of fragrant flowers bloom most

Seagrape (*Coccoloba uvifera*).
Photo by the author.

abundantly in the spring, but some flowers are produced nearly year-round. Showy clusters of juicy, reddish purple fruit, ¾–1 inch in diameter, are most abundant in late summer. The size of the fruit limits their use to mammals and larger birds. Like the fruit of its close cousin, described above, these fruit are edible and sometimes used to make jelly.

Pines

If any group of plants characterizes natural Florida, it is the pines (*Pinus* spp.). Many of Florida's most widespread plant communities are dominated by pines, and the communities are named for their most common species of pine; thus, the state has slash pine flatwoods, longleaf pine sandhills, and sand pine scrubs. Pines grow all over Florida and occur in most habitat types. Their wide-spreading crowns, strong limbs, and evergreen needles provide excellent wildlife cover. Even after they die, pines are a favored nesting tree for many species of animals. Pines are monoecious. Pine seeds, usually ¼–½ inch long, are quite nutritious and eaten by many birds and small mammals. Some animals even chew the unripe cones to get at the seeds before the cones open. Like the oaks, pines vary in the amount of seed produced, and some skip years between good seed crops. Cones ripen the second year after they form, and the seeds generally are dispersed in the fall. Pines also are significant to insect-eating birds and lizards. Their flaky and often deeply fissured bark provides ideal sites for beetles and other insects to seek refuge. The next time you're in a pineland, watch to see where the feeding activity is. More often than not, it is happening along the trunks and branches of the mature pines. Pines are also the host plants for many moths. Moth larvae can be a significant food source for nestling birds as well as many adults. Finally, pine needles provide an ideal mulch both for aesthetic reasons and for the production of invertebrates. While our neighbors are raking and bagging the needles of their pines each fall, Alexa and I are asking their permission to haul the bagged needles home to our front-yard pineland. If you have pine needles or have access to them, do not send them to a landfill. Use them around your plantings.

Sand pine (*Pinus clausa*). Photo by the author.

Sand Pine (*Pinus clausa*)

Sand pine is a medium-sized tree (rarely exceeding 70 feet) native to deep, well-drained, sandy habitats of north and central Florida. The thin 2–3½-inch needles occur in bundles of two and give the tree a kind of feathery appearance. Sand pines grow quickly but are generally not long lived. I have also found them to be extremely sensitive to growing conditions and easily killed. The cones persist on the tree, often for many years, remaining closed until after a fire. This trait allows this species to colonize burned areas quickly but reduces its value as a wildlife food tree. A sand pine variety that does not need fire to open its cones is available and would be a better choice for the wildlife landscape.

Slash Pine (*P. elliottii*)

Slash pine is the state's most widely distributed pine, occurring statewide in a variety of habitats. Its name is derived from the practices of the turpentine industry, once vitally important to the state's economy. The tree trunks were slashed and the dripping sap was collected to be distilled into turpentine and other naval stores. Slash pines produce large and regular seed crops that are important wildlife food. Their 5–11-inch, rigid needles, in bundles of two or three, provide good cover. Slash pines are drought tolerant and well adapted to all but the most excessively drained, sandy Florida soils. They can also tolerate periodic flooding of short duration and are relatively salt tolerant. Two varieties occur in Florida: var. *elliottii*, occurring in north and central Florida, has an open, irregular crown; var.

Slash pine (*Pinus elliottii*). Photo by the author.

densa occurs in central and south Florida and has a more rounded crown, denser needles, and slower growth rate. "Improved" strains of the former, promoted by some agencies, are good for quick timber production, but their lack of lower branches limits their wildlife cover value.

Spruce Pine (*P. glabra*)

Spruce pine is not widely grown commercially nor often planted in the landscape. This is regrettable as this pine has much to recommend it. Spruce pine is a fast-growing, rather large (to 100 feet) tree native to upland forests in north and north central Florida. In areas around Gainesville, for example, it is a common component of the mixed-forest community. I have planted it well into central Florida with good success, but it is not adaptable beyond this range. Its name is derived from its distinctive nonflaky bark that looks similar to that of spruces (*Picea* spp.). Spruce pine has a rather

Spruce pine (*Pinus glabra*). Photo by Shirley Denton, with permission.

narrow, open crown and short (2–3-inch) slender needles in clusters of two. The cones are small, but seed production is regular.

Longleaf Pine (*P. palustris*)

Longleaf pine (*Pinus palustris*).
Photo by the author.

Longleaf pine is a large (to 120 feet), long-lived tree found in a variety of upland habitats from north to south central Florida. As its name implies, its needles (in clusters of three) are extremely long; 15 inches and more in length. These are mostly clustered at the tips of the branches and add to the tree's distinctive appearance. The stout branches and long, dense needles make it an excellent wildlife cover tree, and its relatively flat crown provides a good platform for nesting raptors and wading birds. Longleaf pine produces the largest cones of any native pine, and the seeds are an important source of wildlife food. Good cone production occurs only every three to four years (or more). Longleaf pine is often considered slow growing, because it devotes most of its energy during its first three to seven years to developing a long taproot. Once this is accomplished, its rate of upward growth is quick. Specimens should be grown (and purchased) in long cones or tubelings so their taproots do not become hopelessly coiled. Pot-bound trees with taproots coiled in spirals around the bottom of the pot will not develop stable root systems unless the roots are pruned back cleanly and then forced to redevelop. Longleaf pine is very adaptable to growing conditions (although it prefers well-drained soil) and has good salt tolerance.

Loblolly pine (*Pinus taeda*). Photo by Shirley Denton, with permission.

Loblolly Pine/Oldfield Pine (*P. taeda*)

Loblolly pine is Florida's largest pine, often reaching 120 feet in height. It is quick to establish in disturbed sites; hence one of its common names. Loblolly pine is native to fertile soil habitats in north and north-central Florida, although it is sometimes planted successfully in south-central regions. When young, this pine somewhat resembles the slash pine, but the loblolly has shorter needles, always with three per sheath. As it matures, it can also be identified by its large, straight trunk and spiny cones. This is an adaptable tree that produces large seed crops and good cover for wildlife. It is more susceptible than other pines, however, to damage from southern pine beetles and fusiform rust disease, which may manifest itself more in urban areas, where additional stresses occur, or in the southern edge of its range, where winters are mild.

Privets

Privets (*Forestiera* spp.), are sometimes referred to as wild olives, and they belong to the same family as the other native "wild olives" (*Osmanthus* spp.) as well as the true olives. Privets, however, are small-leaved, multi-stemmed shrubs. Rather small flowers are produced in abundance along the stems in late winter or early spring. Their strong fragrance is somewhat like overripe fruit, and they attract a diverse variety of pollinating flies, in addition to bees and butterflies. Their small purple fruit are ripe by late spring. Because they ripen well before those of most other native plants, these fruit are especially important to songbirds and small mammals. Although several native species in this genus occur in Florida, only one is widely grown and commercially available.

Florida Privet/Wild Olive (*F. segregata*)

Florida privet is an evergreen shrub of coastal dune and hammock habitats throughout peninsular Florida. It is exceedingly adaptable to every growing condition and can be used in a very wide range of landscape settings. It also adapts well to shearing, so it makes an ideal addition to a more formal hedge. Quick growing, Florida privet will eventually reach

Florida privet (*Forestiera segregata*). Photo by the author.

about 15 feet in height. If pruned, it will become denser than if left to grow naturally. Regardless, its branches are rather thin, providing only average nesting cover, but good hiding cover for songbirds and other small wildlife. Florida privet is dioecious, so only the females produce the large and dependable crops of ¼-inch purple fruit that make this such a valuable wildlife plant. Though numerous insects are drawn to the blooms in early spring, it is not an important larval food plant for moths and butterflies, and the foliage is not especially significant to browsing wildlife such as deer and rabbits. Use this plant as part of a hedge, even in coastal situations, or as part of an understory planting. Because it is dioecious, it needs to be planted in groups.

Sassafras

Sassafras (*Sassafras albidum*) is a member of the bay family and may become a 60–70-foot tree, although it is normally much smaller. This attractive, deciduous, dioecious species is native to sandy, well-drained, open habitats of north and north central Florida. It does not perform well south of its natural range and should not be used there. Flowers of both sexes are lemon yellow and attractive. The variable leaves are often mitten or trident shaped and turn red, orange, and yellow in the fall. The ½-inch purplish fruit ripen by early fall on the female trees and are eaten by songbirds and small mammals. Good fruit production occurs only every two to three years. Sassafras is the larval food plant of several moths and the spicebush swallowtail butterfly. Plant it in open areas in a small grouping to make sure you get at least one of each sex. Oils from the bark are used to make sassafras tea. Sassafras has only minimal salt tolerance and should not be used in coastal plantings.

Sassafras (*Sassafras albidum*). Photo by Shirley Denton, with permission.

Spicewoods and Stoppers

The true myrtles (not to be confused with the wax myrtles) are one of the largest families of flowering plants worldwide, with the majority tropical in distribution. All species native to the United States occur in south Florida and have only marginal tolerance to cold temperatures. All our species are small to medium-sized evergreen shrubs with simple, often aromatic leaves and small fleshy fruit. They are monoecious and highly salt tolerant. The flowers are white, often fragrant, and attractive. All are tolerant of shade, salt, and alkaline soil. Members of this family provide moderate wildlife cover, but birds and other wildlife greatly favor the fruit. Non-native members of this family include Surinam cherry (*Eugenia uniflora*) and the various species of guavas (*Psidium* spp.). Because of their attractiveness to birds, the non-native species are often serious invasive problems in the natural areas of south Florida. There are two native spicewoods and five stoppers. Several are very rare and not included in this discussion; the others are widely available and discussed below in more detail. The stoppers (*Eugenia* spp.) are so named because their leaves were used by early settlers as a remedy for diarrhea. The leaves of members of

Spicewood (*Calyptranthes pallens*). Photo by the author.

this genus emit a skunklike odor, and the shrubs can be detected in the woods well before they are seen. For this reason, they may not be your best choice for areas near windows you frequently open. Stoppers are a common component of the understory of south Florida coastal and hardwood hammocks because they are adaptable and because their great fruit production is widely dispersed in the droppings of birds.

Spicewood (*Calyptranthes pallens*)

Spicewood occurs throughout south Florida. Seldom exceeding 20 feet in height, it is an attractive shrub with arching branches tipped with rusty-colored new growth. Clusters of small, nonshowy flowers bloom in early summer, and the reddish, ¼-inch fruit ripen to black by fall. These are consumed mostly by birds. Spicewood grows best in partial shade in moist soil. Its tolerance to cold has not been well documented, and it is best used only in frost-free areas of the state. In these locations, use this interesting shrub as a component of a mixed-species hammock landscape. Flowering and fruiting will be greatly enhanced, however, if it is not grown in conditions too shady.

White Stopper (*Eugenia axillaris*)

White stopper is a widely distributed stopper, occurring well into central Florida along the east and west coasts. Named for its light-colored bark, it may reach 25 feet in height. New growth is reddish, and the leaves are elliptical with pointed tips. Flowering occurs in summer, and the ⅓-inch, reddish fruit ripen to black by fall. The

White stopper (*Eugenia axillaris*). Photo by the author.

foliage of this plant is extremely aromatic, more than that of the others. This species is best used in small clusters instead of as specimens. In such a setting, the dense foliage compensates for the narrow crown and relatively thin branches, and cover value is greatly enhanced.

Spanish Stopper (*E. foetida*)

Spanish stopper is a 15–20-foot shrubby tree with rather small, rounded, aromatic leaves. Despite its scientific name, I have not found its foliage nearly as pungent as that of white stopper. Flowering occurs in the summer, and the ¼-inch blackish fruit ripen by late fall. Spanish stopper tolerates cold temperatures into the upper 20s Fahrenheit and can be used in coastal landscapes as far north as Pinellas County on the west coast and Brevard County on the east.

Spanish stopper (*Eugenia foetida*). Photo by the author.

Simpson Stopper/Twinberry Stopper (*Myrcianthes fragrans*)

Simpson stopper is a close relative of the *Eugenia* species of stoppers described above, but is more cold tolerant and adaptable to a wider range

Simpson stopper (*Myrcianthes fragrans*). Photo by the author.

of landscape settings. In addition, its foliage lacks a skunklike odor. As a component of the shady understory of a hammock forest, Simpson stopper is a thin-trunked narrow-crowned tree that can reach 20 feet at maturity. When grown in sunnier locations, it stays much shorter and fuller and tends to act more like a shrub. In either setting, the small rounded leaves and flaky reddish bark are distinctive. The rather stiff branches give this species better overall cover and nesting value for wildlife than its relatives, and this is especially true for specimens grown in sunnier locations. The scientific name is derived from the numerous white, very fragrant flowers produced in a mass across the entire crown of the plant. Flowering is most common in the early spring but often occurs at other times when summer rains are reliable and conditions are good. The bright red, ⅓-inch fruit ripen several months after flowering and are quickly eaten by birds and some small mammals. They are also edible for human consumption. Simpson stopper is one of the most adaptable and useful plants for wildlife landscaping in central and south Florida. It makes an interesting specimen planting or hedge in areas where it will receive sun. As part of a woodland understory, its red flaky bark is accented and lends beauty that is not as apparent in sunnier settings. Flowering and fruiting, however, will not be as abundant.

Strongbarks

Strongbarks (*Bourreria* spp.) are native only to south Florida; they are limited to this region by lack of cold tolerance. Despite their limited range, they are useful additions to the wildlife landscape. Strongbarks are notable for their many clusters of fragrant white flowers, most abundant in the summer and fall, and their abundant round, ½-inch, orange-red fruit that ripen mostly in the fall and early winter. The flowers attract hummingbirds, butterflies, and pollinating insects, and the fruit provide food to many birds and small mammals. All of Florida's species are monoecious. They also are evergreen, with oval leaves 1–3 inches wide, relatively dense branches, and rapid growth. Because of these features, they have value as wildlife cover. Strongbarks are tolerant of alkaline soils. They are best grown in partial shade in a mixed-species woodland planting or

as accent shrubs where their many aesthetic qualities can be admired. Renowned Florida naturalist Roger Hammer adds that the common name "strongbark" is really a corruption of "strongback," the name used by native Bahamians for this family of plants and for the leaf tea prepared in the Bahamas for "weakness and pains of the waistline" and as a sexual aid "to give men a strong back."

Although several species occur in Florida, only one, Bahama strongbark (*B. succulenta*) is commonly available in the nursery trade. It is a shrubby tree that sometimes reaches 25 feet in height but is usually 10–15 feet tall. Bahama strongbark has moderate salt tolerance.

Bahama strongbark (*Bourreria succulenta*). Photo by Roger Hammer, with permission.

Sumacs

The sumacs are a family of shrubs and small trees represented by many economically important species, including the mango (*Mangifera indica*), cashew (*Anacardium occidentale*), and pistachio (*Pistacia vera*), and a variety of widespread "weeds" such as the introduced Brazilian pepper or "Florida holly" (*Schinus terebinthifolius*). Many sumac species, including poison ivy (*Toxicodendron radicans*) and poison oak (*Toxicodendron pubescens*), produce a milky sap that is either poisonous or irritating to humans. Although many sumacs have value as wildlife plants, only one can be recommended for the home landscape.

Winged Sumac/Shiny Sumac (*Rhus copallinum*)

Winged sumac occurs throughout Florida in a wide variety of soils and habitats. Unlike many of its relatives, this shrub does not produce allergic reactions in most people. Often occurring as a thicket-forming shrub, it may reach 25 feet in height under good growing conditions, but is often much shorter. This is a fast-growing, short-lived species with a tendency

Winged sumac (*Rhus copallinum*). Photo by the author.

to spread through the landscape by root suckers; therefore, it is difficult to control in a landscape and best used where it can be contained by walkways or regular mowing, or in areas allowed to "naturalize." It also prefers sunny areas and can be controlled by shade. One of its landscape attributes is its brilliant red fall color. Its common names are derived from its shiny green leaves and the winglike appendages along its leaf stalks, or petioles. Winged sumac flowers in midsummer, and its numerous ⅛-inch reddish fruit are available by fall to the many songbirds that feed on them. It is monoecious and produces dependable fruit crops each year. Uneaten fruit will persist on the plant well into winter, making them even more valuable to birds such as cedar waxwings and American robins. The foliage is relished by rabbits and white-tailed deer. Winged sumac has only marginal salt tolerance and is not an especially good choice for coastal landscapes.

Sweetgum

Sweetgum (*Liquidambar styraciflua*) is a member of the witch-hazel family and the only one commonly planted in landscapes. It is a straight-trunk, deciduous, narrow-crowned tree that can reach more than 120 feet in height. Native to north and central regions of Florida, it is abundant in wet and poorly drained soils as well as in well-drained upland sites, and adaptable to nearly every landscape setting within the northern two-thirds of the state. Overall, sweetgum is not an especially important wildlife plant. The tall, strongly branched trees provide good cover in their narrow canopy, but the flattened, ⅓-inch hard seeds produced in numerous very spiny seed balls have minimal food value to songbirds and small mammals. Sweetgum is monoecious. Sweetgum foliage is eaten by a number of insects that provide food for some birds. Most notably, it is the larval food plant for the beautiful luna moth. In central Florida especially, care should be taken to use specimens grown from local sources, as out-of-state stock rarely performs well. Sweetgum can be used as a specimen tree. Because of its narrow crown, it also works well in a woodland with other species in the canopy. Sweetgum has moderate salt tolerance. In the fall, its leaves turn a variety of colors, including deep burgundy, orange, red, and yellow.

Sweetgum (*Liquidambar styraciflua*). Photo by the author.

Tupelos

This is a very small family of woody plants found only in eastern North America and in China, but it contains a very important genus of native plants important to wildlife, the tupelos (*Nyssa* spp.). Florida's tupelos have small, dense clusters of nonshowy, fragrant flowers in the spring and clusters of rather large fruit that ripen by fall. The flowers are especially attractive to pollinating insects, and tupelo honey is renowned worldwide for its flavor and cooking qualities. Tupelos are often dominant components of forested wetland communities. Their large straight trunks and strong branches provide excellent wildlife cover, and their fruit are eagerly consumed by many species of songbirds as well as by small and medium-sized mammals. Although these are generally wetland trees, they are quite adaptable to most typical landscape conditions. Tupelos do not have much tolerance of salt, however. This group contains species that are both monoecious and dioecious. All are deciduous.

Water tupelo (*Nyssa aquatica*). Photo by Shirley Denton, with permission.

Water Tupelo (*N. aquatica*)

Water tupelo is a large tree (to 100 feet) resident to various forested wetlands in north Florida. It can be grown fairly successfully, however, into much of central Florida, and specimens I planted in Pinellas County have done well over the past 20 years. The 3–4-inch-wide oval leaves have slightly toothed margins, and they turn a brilliant red in the fall. Water tupelo produces clusters of both male and female flowers on the same tree. The purple fruit, 1–1½ inches in length, are produced in abundance each fall. This tree is an excellent choice for plantings at the edges of lakes and retention ponds, in situations where bald cypress might also be used.

Ogeechee lime (*Nyssa ogeche*). Photo by the author.

Ogeechee Lime (*N. ogeche*)

Ogeechee lime is a medium-sized tree (to about 50 feet in height) found primarily in the river swamps of north Florida. It also grows sporadically in central Florida and can be used effectively everywhere in the northern half of the state. This tupelo is not widely available and is another native that should be more frequently considered. Its numerous erect branches and oval, 4–6-inch leaves provide good nesting and hiding cover, and its vivid fall color, ranging from purplish to scarlet, makes it aesthetically attractive. Ogeechee lime is dioecious. The large, 1½-inch bright red, acidic fruit ripen by summer and can be used as a lime substitute or made into preserves. Their large size limits their use by birds, but mammals readily eat them. Ogeechee lime is a beautiful addition to a wetland forest planting, but should be planted in groupings to ensure production of fruit.

Blackgum (*N. sylvatica*)

Blackgum is the most widely distributed of our three native tupelos and the most adaptable to landscapes. It is a very large tree (to 120 feet). Two forms generally are recognized: *N. sylvatica* var. *sylvatica* occurs in upland sites in north and central Florida, whereas *N. sylvatica* var. *biflora* is typically a wetland forest resident found throughout the northern two-thirds of the state. Although both forms are distinct from each other from a landscape perspective, they are identical from the perspective of wildlife. This long-lived tree is similar in shape and cover value to water tupelo; the oval-shaped leaves lack teeth and turn brilliant red in the fall—even in central Florida. Blackgum is dioecious. The spring flowers form ½-inch, dark blue fruit by fall that are a favorite wildlife food. Blackgum can be used as a shade tree or planted as part of a mixed-species woodland in upland or wetland settings.

Blackgum/Tupelo (*Nyssa sylvatica*). Photo by the author.

Viburnums

Viburnums (*Viburnum* spp.) are a genus of deciduous shrubs with opposite leaves. Five species are native to Florida, and most are commercially available and excellent additions to the wildlife landscape. As a rule, viburnums are native to mixed woodland plant communities and prefer fertile, moist soils. In cultivation, most are quite adaptable and tolerate a range of soil and light conditions. Showy white clusters of flowers appear in the spring or early summer and the ¼–⅓-inch purplish fruit ripen by late summer or early fall. Viburnums are monoecious and have no salt tolerance.

Southern Arrowwood (*V. dentatum*)

Southern arrowwood is a multi-stemmed shrub with a natural range extending from north Florida to Hernando County. It is a highly variable species but rarely exceeds 9 feet in height. Although adaptable to a broad range of growing conditions, it is best used as an understory shrub in a mixed-woodland setting. I have seen southern arrowwood used successfully in several south-central Florida landscapes, but pushing it much beyond its natural range seems a bit unnecessary as other viburnums may be better choices farther south. Southern arrowwood gets its name from its abundant arrow-straight stems. The leaves are large, with sharply toothed margins. Greenish white flowers

Arrowwood viburnum (*Viburnum dentatum*). Photo by the author.

appear in late spring and early summer. The numerous blue-black fruit ripen by fall. They are especially attractive to a wide variety of songbirds and a few small mammals. The foliage is sometimes eaten by browsing mammals such as white-tailed deer.

Possumhaw (*V. nudum*)

Possumhaw is a large shrub that can reach 15 feet in height. It occurs in wet to moist soils throughout north and central Florida, but is adaptable to average soils in cultivation. Possumhaw has simple, oval-shaped leaves and relatively weak branches that limit its value as nesting cover for songbirds. When planted as an understory shrub in a mixed-woodland landscape, however, its value as other types of cover is enhanced. Possumhaw excels as a source of wildlife food. Its large flower heads,

Possumhaw viburnum (*Viburnum nudum*).
Photo by the author.

which appear in late spring, attract a wide assortment of pollinating insects and produce abundant crops of deep blue fruit in the fall.

Walter's Viburnum (*V. obovatum*)

Walter's viburnum is the most adaptable, widely distributed, and commercially available native viburnum in Florida. This densely branched,

Walter's viburnum (*Viburnum obovatum*). Photo by the author.

shrubby tree, which may reach 30 feet in height, occurs in a variety of moist soil habitats from the central Panhandle to parts of south Florida. Although many references describe this viburnum as evergreen, it loses most or all of its small dark green leaves for a brief period in the winter. Nevertheless, it is one of the best shrubs for wildlife cover because its branches are dense and rigid. Walter's viburnum occurs naturally in moist forest soil habitats, but it is extremely adaptable and quite tolerant of nearly every growing condition once established. Specimens grown in shady locations will be lankier than those in full sun and produce far fewer flowers and fruit. For this reason, it is best used in sunny to mostly sunny locations within a mixed hedge or thicket, or as a specimen planting where its flowers can be easily seen and admired. Walter's viburnum responds well to shearing and makes a nice addition to a managed hedge as well as a naturalized setting. The one drawback to this species is its tendency to spread by root suckers. This can be a problem in areas where its suckering would be difficult to control. Several horticultural varieties are commercially available, including dwarf and compact-growing forms. Walter's viburnum has a smaller inflorescence (cyme) than Florida's other native species, but their sheer numbers make this shrub quite stunning in the spring. The flattened, elliptical fruit, ripening from red to black, are available in early fall and eaten by a wide variety of songbirds.

Rusty Viburnum/Southern Blackhaw (*V. rufidulum*)

Rusty viburnum is a shrub or shrubby tree that may reach 20 feet in height. Its preferred habitats are on fertile, well-drained soils, and it occurs naturally in north and north central Florida. It can be fairly easily grown in many landscape settings well into south central Florida and is quite tolerant of alkaline soils. Its rounded, 2–3-inch, slightly toothed leaves are so glossy they almost look wet. In the fall, they turn a variety of hues, including red, purple, orange, and yellow. Flower heads are scattered across the plant in loose clusters and appear after the leaves have developed in late spring. These are followed by large purplish black fruit in the fall. This is a beautiful shrub for partly shady areas in a naturalized woodland landscape and should be used more than it currently is.

Rusty viburnum (*Viburnum rufidulum*). Photo by the author.

Wax Myrtles

The three species of wax myrtles (*Myrica* spp.) native to Florida are dioecious evergreen shrubs with fairly simple, elliptical leaves and small waxy fruit. They are a valuable group of plants for several reasons: wax myrtles can grow in poor soils and improve them because their roots contain nitrogen-fixing bacteria, much like legumes; their dense branching and foliage create excellent wildlife cover; and the numerous ⅙-inch fruit provide food for many songbirds. The myrtle warbler (now known as the yellow-rumped warbler) was named for its affinity for wax myrtle fruit, but tree swallows also consume them in great numbers in the winter months. The waxy coating on the fruit is the source of bayberry wax, used to scent candles and soaps. Wax myrtles are fast growing but not long lived. The small inconspicuous flowers are produced in the spring, and the dry fruit ripen on female plants by late summer or early fall. Only one species is generally commercially available.

Southern Wax Myrtle (*M. cerifera*)

Southern wax myrtle is one of the most widely grown native shrubs in Florida. It occurs naturally throughout the state in a variety of habitats, from areas of wet soils to upland sites in full sun and semishaded woodlands. It has very good tolerance of salts and is frequently encountered in coastal habitats as well. Southern wax myrtle grows quickly to its mature height of about 20 feet and begins to produce fruit at a very early age. A distinct dwarf variety, *M. cerifera* var. *pumila*, occurs in dry pinelands and remains at about 3 feet in height. Both forms spread slowly by root suckers if allowed. Southern wax myrtle is excellent as a hedge or thicket, because it responds well to shearing. The crushed leaves

Southern wax myrtle (*Myrica cerifera*). Photo by the author.

are aromatic. It can be used as a specimen plant, much the same way the non-native ligustrum is sometimes planted, or it can be effectively incorporated into a mixed hedge or more formal buffer planting.

White Indigoberry (*Randia aculeata*)

White indigoberry is a member of the coffee family, described previously, and shares many of the traits discussed for the coffees and firebush. It is a somewhat thorny, evergreen, 6–10-foot shrub of south and central Florida. Its branches are rather stiff and sturdy, and mature specimens provide good cover for a variety of small songbirds and other wildlife. Though young plants are rather slow growers, they produce fragrant white flowers at an early age. White indigoberry can bloom nearly every month of the year, but flowers are most common in the spring. This is a dioecious species, so only the females produce the elliptical ⅓-inch white-skinned fruit that are its namesake. The bright white skins surround a deep purple flesh that can stain sidewalks and other structures. For this reason, it is

White indigoberry (*Randia aculeata*). Photo by the author.

best to use this plant away from sensitive features where staining would be a problem. White indigoberry is an attractive, adaptable, and useful shrub. Its high tolerance of salt makes it especially useful for coastal landscapes, and its size and sturdiness make it an ideal shrub for hedges and thickets. Use this plant in sunny locations, but do not attempt it in landscapes where winter temperatures typically dip below the mid 20s Fahrenheit.

Wild Cinnamons

Cinnamon bark is the only native member of a small family of tropical evergreen trees, the wild cinnamons. These are not related to the true cinnamons, used as spices, but have a somewhat similar fragrant bark.

Cinnamon Bark (*Canella winterana*)

Cinnamon bark is a small, slow-growing tree that eventually reaches 30 feet in height. It begins to flower and produce fruit at a relatively early age. As its name implies, its bark smells like cinnamon when bruised.

Wild cinnamon (*Canella winterana*). Photo by the author.

Although its natural range in Florida is restricted to coastal woodlands in the Florida Keys and the extreme southern peninsula, it has some cold tolerance and has survived extremely well for the past 20 years in a landscape I planted in Pinellas County that has dipped periodically into the mid-20s Fahrenheit. The dense, rounded crown of this tree and its rather large, thick, aromatic leaves give it good value as wildlife hiding cover, but the relatively thin branches do not provide much for nesting. Trees produce large numbers of maroon-colored flowers in midsummer, and the small clusters of ½-inch, round, bright red fruit ripen in winter, but often persist until early spring. They are eaten by a variety of birds and small mammals. Cinnamon bark is monoecious. This beautiful small tree has much potential for south Florida landscapes in both sunny and partly shady areas. Place it in the landscape where its beautiful flowers and fruit can be noticed.

Wild Lime

Wild lime (*Zanthoxylum fagara*) is not a citrus-type lime (although they are members of the same family), but a prickly ash, and it shares the characteristics of this genus with other members, such as the toothache tree (*Z. clava-herculis*). Wild lime is a small (20–25 feet) evergreen tree with a short trunk and thin, wide-spreading branches. The branches are well armed with small hooked thorns that greatly enhance its wildlife cover value. The highly aromatic leaves comprise 7–15 small rounded leaflets that give it a sort of "lacey" appearance. As a member of the citrus family, this plant serves as a host for the caterpillars of the giant and Schaus' swallowtail butterflies. Few other insects feed on it, however. Wild lime is dioecious. The greenish yellow flowers bloom primarily in the spring and attract a variety of pollinating insects. The flowers are followed by small hard seeds (on the female plant only) that ripen by late summer or early fall. The seeds have only very minor value to most wildlife. Wild lime is native to central and south Florida and can be planted in a wide variety of landscape settings. It has a high tolerance of salt spray as well as of drought. Use this small picturesque tree as a specimen, or incorporate

Wild lime (*Zanthoxylum fagara*). Photo by the author.

it into a mixed planting where it will receive sun. Wild lime will not perform well if given too much shade. Because of its thorniness, it should be
planted well away from walkways and other locations where you might
accidentally stumble into it.

6

Landscape Design

We have discussed the concepts of wildlife habitat, examined the habitat needs of some of the common wildlife for which we might wish to provide habitat, and taken a rather in-depth look at the best native trees and shrubs for our purposes. Landscaping for wildlife habitat requires a full understanding of all these topics before we sit down to plan an actual landscape design. Landscape planning is the whole of the parts. Landscape design is the phase of landscape planning when we decide exactly where each plant will be planted.

Each plant has a certain set of attributes you can use to advantage to create wildlife habitat. Sometimes, plants can contribute most of these attributes on their own, without the assistance of the rest of the landscape, but in the majority of situations, it is the context of the landscape that fully actualizes the role each plant will play in the community you create. As I stated previously, you are not establishing a collection of plants, but a community. Plants work together to provide wildlife habitat, and their individual roles are enhanced by what is planted around them. It is clearly a situation where the whole is greater than the sum of its parts.

You can make up for weaknesses in the cover value of many valuable food plants, for example, by planting these species in a mass or by planting better cover plants nearby. A single wild coffee has little to offer, but a mass of coffees planted under a shady woodland overstory provides excellent hiding cover as well as an abundant source of insects and fruit. A fringetree planted in the open lawn as an accent tree is beautiful but provides little else. The same tree planted in front of an evergreen hedge of wax myrtle and viburnum can be a valuable food source that is now a

A landscape designed for wildlife does not have to ignore aesthetics. This landscape uses both native and non-native plants quite effectively. Photo by the author.

safe shelter for wildlife and birds. As the old real estate adage goes, "it's location, location, location."

As I've also discussed, different wildlife species require different landscape conditions. While most warblers are comfortable only in a woodland setting, purple martins and bluebirds require landscapes that are far more open. Your landscape design will determine the wildlife that eventually use it. It is not only the insects and fruit provided by your plants but also the overall landscape design that play the most important roles in your success at creating habitat.

To be completely successful at creating a community and not just a collection of plants, you need to select species that work together. Generally, that means selecting plants for your landscape that tend to grow together in nature. At a minimum, it means building communities from plants with very similar growing requirements. Plants with similar adaptations to soil, moisture, and sunlight conditions can work together; otherwise, components of the landscape will likely fail and perish. Experimentation is not bad, but it should be done with enough knowledge to make success likely. It is much more difficult to start over than to start correctly.

It is not my purpose in this book to provide you with specific landscape designs. I believe that everybody must come to a personal design based on specific needs, desires, and growing conditions. By copying a plan designed for some theoretical place and purpose, you deprive yourself of the rewards of the creative process and limit yourself to the plants and wildlife chosen by someone else. There is no single landscape plan, and no single correct way to arrive at one. There is, however, a correct way to begin.

If we look to nature for a reference point, we can better understand the various elements of Florida's diverse natural communities. You can use this knowledge as a starting point on the path to a final landscape design. In the pages that follow, I examine some of Florida's most significant plant communities with the purpose of making you more effective at landscape design.

As we examine these communities, realize that your overall landscape design can incorporate more than one of them. While it might make sense to design your entire property as one community, such as a shady woodland, it might be equally sensible not to. It is perfectly acceptable to design a landscape around more than one community, as long as two major concepts are followed: (1) Do not create such small patches of any type of plant that it loses its function. Postage-stamp plantings will not provide habitat if they are not large enough to satisfy the food, water, and cover needs of wildlife. (2) Do not mix communities together. If you design for a shady woodland in one part of the landscape, keep it separate from an open sunny grassland planting you wish to use elsewhere. Each community needs a separate identity to work properly.

NATIVE COMMUNITIES

Study the structure of natural communities and the common species that compose them to increase your chance of success. Each community is unique in both structure and plant components. As you examine natural communities, seek to copy their structure in your plan. The plants themselves occur together in nature because they share similar growing requirements. They provide a good model from which to start, but you can alter it if you choose plants that share a common ability to prosper under the growing conditions you are designing. You might wish to substitute a Walter's viburnum for a Florida privet, for example, when either will work, although you might never find both growing side by side in nature. Your goal is not necessarily to re-create a natural community plant by plant. This objective can work well, but it is not necessary. Build a landscape plan with plants that will function together and provide the food and cover characteristics your wildlife need, and choose a structure based on one of Florida's natural communities.

Natural communities in Florida vary considerably, depending on elevation, soil structure, and soil fertility. These forces sometimes alter the structure of the community, but more often they alter only the composition of the plants. Therefore, it is possible to have dense shady forests (hammocks) on well-drained xeric soils as well as on moist fertile ones. Open grass-dominated prairies can occur on seasonally flooded areas and on areas that rarely have standing water. The structure of coastal hammocks is very similar to that of inland hammocks. The differences arise from degrees of tolerance to salt. As long as the plants you choose match your growing conditions, you are on the way to building a community.

What follows are descriptions of some of Florida's most common plant communities. Descriptions and photographs are provided to give you a better idea of how these communities develop and what their structure looks like. It is my hope that you will be able to use this information to develop a landscape design. Each community description includes a list of some associated trees and shrubs described in this book. The letter in parentheses following each plant name roughly defines the part of the state where it grows best: (A) = can be grown in all parts of the state, except the Keys; (N) = can be grown in the Panhandle and the northern half of the peninsula; (S) = can be grown in the southern half of the peninsula and the Keys. These lists are intended only as examples of the types of plants that are part of each community. I have not identified specific plants adapted only to the Florida Keys.

Dunes and Scrubs

Dunes and scrubs occur on excessively well-drained sands; they are characterized by a general lack of overstory trees and an understory of widely spaced woody and herbaceous plants with bare sand between them. In fact, the bare sands play a significant role for many of the wildlife species residing in these systems, both for burrowing and for caching (burying) food items such as acorns. Many of Florida's most unique and interesting wildlife require these conditions, and some of our most beautiful and interesting plants are found nowhere else. A scrub or dune garden can

An example of a dune community, Topsail Hill Preserve State Park, Okaloosa County. Photo by the author.

An example of a Florida scrub community, Polk County. Photo by the author.

be created anywhere with very well-drained, sandy soil. If you choose plants wisely, you will not have to irrigate or fertilize these areas, except during periods of extreme drought or to get new plants established—and, under these conditions, weeds will have a hard time gaining a foothold. The open white (or yellow) sand between your plants will be aesthetically pleasing, and maintenance of the plantings should be minimal.

Besides the need for deep sandy soils, dune and scrub plantings should be attempted only in areas of full sun. Do not try to establish this community in areas where trees or shrubs shade it for more than a small part of the day. Be careful, too, that you don't plant too densely or use plants in small spaces that spread rapidly. Plants such as railroad vine (*Ipomea pes-caprae*) are beautiful in an expansive dune planting but will overwhelm your other plants if used in a smaller area.

If you choose this landscape approach, you will want to select woody plants very carefully. For the most part, you will be selecting small trees and shrubs that normally grow no taller than 15 feet at maturity. Space these far apart from each other to leave room for understory plantings and to ensure you do not produce too much shade. For a scrub design, good choices include the scrub oaks (myrtle, sand live, and Chapman), pigmy fringetree, and tough bumelia. For a dune planting, you might use such species as prostrate coco plum.

Interspersed between woody plantings, use any number of the beautiful woody or herbaceous wildflowers to provide color and texture, as well as the seeds and nectar useful to wildlife. If you are planting a dune garden, you will want to add some of the nonaggressive bunchgrasses common to this community (e.g., sea oats, *Uniola paniculata*) for additional texture and cover, as well as seeds and foliage. There are few grasses native to the Florida scrub, and you may wish to avoid planting grasses if you wish to adopt this landscape approach. Use the many wonderful wildflowers available to you and be satisfied with them. Some dune wildflowers have a tendency to sprawl and spread. If you choose any of these species, be careful to give them a large enough space or be prepared to do some regular pruning and weeding. Success with these communities is not measured by an increasing density of plants, but by being rather open. The ground needs patches of open, bare sand, or many plants will ultimately fail and you will lose the diversity and character you designed for.

It is difficult to create dune and scrub communities in places where they do not occur naturally. If you happen to own or purchase land that was historically dune or scrub, embrace the opportunities it affords. By reclaiming some of this land for nature, you will have restored habitat that has declined significantly because of urban development. Open sand, with mostly dwarf trees and no lush green grass, is foreign to our traditional landscape aesthetic and an acquired taste, but such an approach can also create some of the most interesting and valuable habitat in the right places.

It is possible to create scrub or dunes where they never occurred, but it takes a great amount of effort and will likely never attract any of the true scrub or dune wildlife you may desire. A scrub habitat will, however,

A portion of my personal dune/scrub landscape, Pinellas County. Wildflowers and low-growing woody shrubs are clearly separated by open sand. Photo by the author.

provide conditions for wildlife that prefer open types of habitat. I created scrub several times in different locations by removing the existing organic sands from the top several feet and replacing with purchased scrub sand. In these conditions, I was able to experiment with a wide range of plant species I may never have been able to grow otherwise, but my experiment was on a small scale.

Scrub Plant Palette

Trees

1. Sand pine (A)
2. Sand live oak (A)
3. Chapman oak (A)
4. Silk bay (N)
5. Scrub hickory (A)

Shrubs

1. Tough bumelia (A)
2. Carolina holly (A)

Dune Plant Palette

Trees

None

Shrubs

1. Coco plum (S)
2. Inkberry (*Scaevola plumieri*) (S)

Prairies

Florida prairies are not quite the same as the grasslands that once dominated much of the central portion of this country, but they share some of the same structural characteristics. They are essentially treeless areas dominated by grasses and wildflowers. In Florida, such communities generally developed in locations that burned so frequently that trees were unable to establish. Frequent fire is necessary for many of these species to fully achieve their potential and reproduce successfully, creating conditions that prevent some species from becoming too large and overwhelming less aggressive ones.

In the home landscape, fire is not normally a viable management option. Although I have friends who contract with the Florida Division of Forestry to regularly burn their yards, it is not something that can be done safely or easily in most home landscape settings. A compromise is occasional mowing. If mowing is done in late winter or early spring with the mower set at approximately 6 inches or higher, it will prevent a home prairie from becoming too thick and allow less aggressive species to coexist with the more aggressive ones.

Prairies are not a landscape approach for small areas. Species such as meadowlarks and burrowing owls generally require expansive areas of open grassland. In smaller areas, such as a typical front yard, a prairie community can provide some wildlife cover for species that prefer open sunny conditions and food for wildlife that feed on grasses and herbaceous plants as well as others that require seeds and insects.

As prairies do not have trees and the few woody shrubs stay small and low to the ground, your landscape will be dependent largely on native grasses and herbaceous wildflowers, plants not covered by this book. Florida has many native grasses, and these form the foundation of a prairie design. For the most part, use the smaller bunch grasses, such as wiregrass (*Aristida* spp.) and pinewoods dropseed (*Sporobolus junceus*), as a foundation, and the taller bunchgrasses, such as the bluestems (*Andropogon* spp.), lop-sided Indiangrass (*Sorghastrum secundum*), and muhly grass (*Muhlenbergia capillaris*) for accents. Herbaceous wildflowers will then be incorporated into this matrix, not the other way around. Use wildflowers that are good seed producers, not just species that are pretty to look

The dry prairie community, Kissimmee Prairie Preserve State Park, Okeechobee County.
Photo by Christina Evans, with permission.

at. Luckily, many of the most beautiful are also useful. Good choices are many in the aster family, for example, sunflowers (*Helianthus* spp.), asters (*Symphyotrichum* spp.), blazing stars (*Liatris* spp.), black-eyed susans (*Rudbeckia* spp.), goldenasters (*Pityopsis* spp.), and coneflowers (*Ratibida* and *Echinacea* spp.) as well as legumes, for example, prairie clover (*Dalea* spp.), wild indigo (*Baptisia* spp.), and partridge pea (*Chamaecrista* spp.).

If designed and maintained correctly, a prairie landscape can be beautiful. If not, it will be an eyesore. To ensure success, maximize diversity, select species that bloom at different times of the year, and manage it so it does not become rank.

Prairie Plant Palette

Trees

None

Shrubs

1. Saw palmetto (A)
2. Dwarf live oak (A)

Sandhills

Sandhills develop on upland sandy soils, subject to frequent fire. Under these conditions, they develop a parklike character with widely spaced canopy trees, very little midcanopy (i.e., woody brush), and a species-rich understory of native grasses and wildflowers. In many respects, a well-managed sandhill is similar to the prairie community, but with an open canopy of trees added. It also is somewhat similar in structure to the traditional developed landscape we see across Florida, because the dominant species in each are the understory plants (grasses and flowers), not trees. It is not a huge leap to move from one to the other. The major change from a traditional landscape to a sandhill design is replacement

An example of a longleaf pine sandhill community, Riverside Island Tract, Ocala National Forest, Marion County. Photo by the author.

of highly manicured, intensively maintained turf grasses and flower beds with a diverse collection of nonturf grasses and wildflowers that are not regularly mowed, watered, and fertilized.

The sandhill understory is diverse because it is not densely shaded by trees. Instead of "shade trees" (e.g., oaks and maples), the canopy is dominated by pines, especially longleaf pine. Pines filter sun but do not completely block it from reaching the ground. Although other trees can do the same if their canopies are not too wide and their branches too dense, pines are the best for this purpose.

Frequent fire under natural conditions prevents woody plants from forming a midcanopy. Under suburban conditions, regular, but infrequent, mowing would do much the same to maintain this structure. Instead of mowing weekly during the growing season, mow once in late winter or early spring, after the grasses and wildflowers have set seed and been dispersed or eaten by wildlife. In addition, set your mower no lower than 6 inches to ensure no harm to the native grasses by mowing too close. Sandhill grasses are bunch grasses, not turf grasses, and they are damaged when the mower cuts into their "heart." By setting the mower above it, you ensure that only the grass blades are cut.

Your understory would look much the same as that described for the prairie. The key species will be grasses, and the most significant will be wiregrass. To increase diversity and structure, you can add several of the taller grasses such as lop-sided Indiangrass, bluestems, and little bluestems. Use taller grasses judiciously, and scatter them no closer than 6 feet apart. Build the main structure from wiregrass.

Lay out the primary pattern of your sandhill understory with native grasses, then fill the remaining spaces with a wide variety of wildflowers, emphasizing species that produce seeds for birds and nectar for insects. Remember to keep an eye on the objective of color for as many months as possible. Some of the best species will be members of the aster family with flower heads tall enough to rise above the grasses. Some of the best are blazing stars (especially *Liatris spicata*, *L. gracilis*, and *L. tenuifolia*), Florida paintbrush (*Carphephorus corymbosus*), resindot sunflower (*Helianthus resinosus*), kidneyleaf rosinweed (*Silphium compositum*), and grass-leaf goldenaster (*Pityopsis graminifolia*).

Once established, the sandhill community requires very little maintenance besides infrequent mowing and weeding. Be careful to prevent aggressive weeds from becoming established that will eventually overwhelm the native species. It is also important not to allow suckering, spreading grasses, such as torpedo grass (*Panicum repens*), to gain a foothold. Because the sandhill understory eventually forms a dense carpet without the patches of open sand common to the dune and scrub communities, weeding out unwelcome species becomes difficult once they become entrenched.

Sandhill Plant Palette

Trees

1. Longleaf pine (N)
2. South Florida slash pine (S)
3. Turkey oak (A)

4. Bluejack oak (A)
5. Post oak (N)
6. Summer haw (N)

Shrubs

1. Gopher apple (A)
2. Saw palmetto (A)
3. Dwarf live oak (A)

Flatwoods

The flatwoods community occurs throughout Florida. It develops on relatively flat lands, and the lack of topography often means that it is wet during the rainy season and rather dry during the late winter and spring. Flatwoods are dominated by a canopy of widely spaced trees (usually a mixture of longleaf and slash pine) but have a well-developed woody subcanopy in addition to the grasses and wildflowers that find a niche among them. As such, natural woody thickets can be found within the community and provide much denser cover than you would find in a sandhill, scrub, or prairie. Well-managed flatwoods, however, are largely open expanses where the shrubby understory is maintained to a height of only a few feet by fire. The flatwoods structure allows light to reach the understory, and a well-managed flatwoods has a wide diversity of native grasses and wildflowers. Patches of denser woody cover create more opportunity for birds, such as the Northern cardinal and eastern towhee, to nest in the midcanopy.

Use this structure as a compromise between the wide open communities described above and the deep shady conditions of a hammock forest, described later. Flatwoods function as they do because the canopy is not too dense to prevent significant sunlight from reaching the ground. Use canopy trees that do not block the sunlight. Pines are good candidates, but other narrow-crowned or open-branched species would provide the same conditions. Beneath this canopy, create woody thickets in key locations to serve as hiding and nesting cover for wildlife. For this objective, you have many choices, but be careful of species that readily sucker or become too large. The key is to combine species with complementary characteristics that will work together, not strive to dominate. Once the woody plants are installed, fill the holes between the shrubby pockets with native grasses and wildflowers. Use smaller species near the front of the landscape and near trails and pathways, and use the taller grasses and wildflowers where they will need to get taller to be noticed.

Natural flatwoods are diverse and provide excellent wildlife habitat when they are managed. In places where fire has been excluded and the woody subcanopy is allowed to grow unchecked, many flatwoods wildlife lose the habitat they require. When designing a flatwoods landscape structure, it is important to manage the areas of woody thickets to prevent them from overrunning the pockets of grasses and herbaceous wildflowers. Occasional and selective pruning will be important. Keep the thicket areas dense, but don't allow them to spread too far. And, take extra care in the first few years to keep unwanted species from gaining a foothold. Birds, in particular, often spread the seeds of invasive species beneath their favorite roosting places. Check thickets regularly to make sure that

An example of a pine flatwoods community, Goethe State Forest, Levy County. Photo by the author.

A portion of the native grass and wildflower area in my personal landscape, Pinellas County. A small island of saw palmetto provides denser cover inside the open sandhill/flatwoods understory planted around it. Photo by the author.

Brazilian pepper, carrotwood (*Cupaniopsis anacardioides*), camphor, and other non-natives are not being planted for you.

Flatwoods Plant Palette

Trees

1. Longleaf pine (N)
2. Slash pine (A)
3. Florida thatch palm (S)

Shrubs

1. Southern wax myrtle (A)
2. Common gallberry (A)
3. Beautyberry (A)
4. Saw palmetto (A)
5. Blueberries (A)
6. Spicewood (S)
7. Locustberry (S)

Hammocks

Hammocks are shady forested habitats. They develop under a wide variety of conditions, assuming different characteristics and comprising vastly different species in different conditions. Depending on conditions found in your landscape, you will want to tailor hammock plantings to species that are adapted.

In lower elevations or adjacent to wetlands, hammocks are composed of species adapted to moist soils. These hydric hammocks often have a dense understory of ferns and a canopy of rather shallow-rooted trees. Commonly encountered species include laurel oak, cabbage palm, sweetbay, red maple, and American elm.

An example of a hydric hammock forest, Torreya State Park, Liberty County. Photo by the author.

An example of mesic hammock forest, Devil's Millhopper Geological State Park, Alachua County. Photo by the author.

Hammocks that develop on average soils are generally referred to as mesic hammocks. Often, these are dominated by deciduous trees. Over time, the leaf litter enhances soil fertility and moderates moisture levels. Mesic hammocks are some of the most diverse systems in Florida, often with many species of ferns and wildflowers in their understory, a rich midcanopy of shrubs and small trees, and a high diversity of canopy species. Some of Florida's most beautiful midcanopy trees (e.g., fringetree, flowering dogwood, silverbell [*Halesia diptera*]) and flowering shrubs (e.g., viburnums) are resident to mesic hammocks. The canopy is dominated by a collection of oaks, hickories, hackberries, southern magnolia, and the like.

In droughty soils and on the tops of ridges, the hammock forest normally loses some of its diversity and is composed of plants better adapted

An example of south Florida coastal hammock forest, Key Largo, Dagny Johnson Key Largo Hammock Botanical State Park. Photo by the author.

to poorer soils and less moisture. These xeric hammocks often have a somewhat open understory with far fewer ferns and a canopy dominated by fewer tree species. Common to this forest are live oak and southern red cedar.

Soil moisture and elevation are not the only driving forces shaping the type of hammock that develops naturally on a site. Hammocks that develop along the coast have their own structure based on the need for salt tolerance, especially salt spray. In extreme south Florida, coastal hammocks also require tolerance of limestone and generally take on a character all their own. Interior hammocks at this latitude do not necessarily need to be able to tolerate salt, but they form on shallow soils above lime rock, and the plants in them must be adapted to high pH, shallow and often droughty soils, and lack of a cold season.

Because we so often use shade trees in landscaping, many of us already have a sort-of-hammock somewhere on our property. Of course, there are vast differences between the structure of a natural hammock and the structure normally created by suburban landscape designers.

Native hammocks typically have a diverse canopy of deciduous and/or evergreen trees, a relatively diverse subcanopy of smaller trees and shrubs, and a far less diverse understory of shade-tolerant herbaceous plants. In temperate hammocks dominated by deciduous trees, a flush of spring-blooming wildflowers often occurs, including violets (*Viola* spp.) and jack-in-the-pulpit (*Arisaema triphyllum*), before the canopy closes over with new leaves. In evergreen hammocks, this component is mostly lacking because insufficient light reaches the ground. In both types, ferns and other shade-tolerant species are common, and open ground fills the spaces between them. This layer of open ground, leaf litter, and decaying limbs and branches provides significant habitat for forest wildlife. The other significant wildlife layer is the canopy.

Native hammocks are diverse and composed of well-defined layers. Shady areas of our yard generally are not. If we wish to make the conversion, we will need to create diversity out of already existing conditions. The first need is to evaluate what is missing. If you already have a good number of oaks, for example, you might want to add other canopy trees that provide different foods and habitat structure. If you have no room for more canopy trees, work on inserting the midcanopy component and the ground covers—in that order.

Most landscapes with shade trees have little beneath the trees besides sickly turf grass. Define where the light gaps are and where you can best plant understory trees and shrubs, giving each some room between the trunks of the canopy trees. Many are spring-blooming species and will add color to the woodland once established. This is especially true if the canopy loses its leaves in late winter/early spring.

A portion of my personal hammock forest, Pinellas County. The canopy is largely live oak left by the developer. A subcanopy and understory were planted underneath to increase diversity and wildlife habitat value. Photo by the author.

After you have installed the overstory and midcanopy, you can look to the ground covers. Realize that the amount of shade in your hammock will increase significantly as your overstory and midcanopy levels develop. Because of this, many species that might eventually flourish will get too much sun to survive if planted at the outset. In my own yard, I have planned for this by planting wildflowers in the sunnier locations while the forest develops, knowing they will eventually have to be replaced by ferns and violets as the canopy closes over. In the shadier locations, I have already used shade-dependent species.

Eventually, your hammock will stabilize and require very little additional effort. Each fall, the canopy will lose its leaves (even most of the "evergreen" species lose their leaves), which will mulch the forest floor. When the hammock is young, you may need to augment this leaf litter by adding leaves from elsewhere. Most of your neighbors may already be raking their leaves for you, bagging them, and putting them on the curb. Ask if you can take the fruit of their labor for your yard, and they will probably be happy to give it away. It may also be beneficial to add some structure to the developing forest floor. Look for logs and large limbs pruned from your neighbors' trees and set out for curbside pick-up. These can add important wildlife cover, and the insects attracted to the decaying wood will provide important sources of food. Do not put such structure next to your home, however, and invite termites to move in.

Even small wooded areas can be important habitat magnets for forest birds. During migration, in particular, my small developing hammock and those of my neighbors provide constant excitement as warblers, vireos, and other songbirds stop by to feed on their way north or south. During the rest of the year, there is always something flitting through the tree tops. By stocking your midcanopy with woody species that produce flowers and fruit, you will be surprised at how many species you provide for—even if some are around for only a few hours each year.

Hydric Hammock

Canopy Trees

1. Bald cypress (A)
2. Blackgum (A)
3. Red maple (A)
4. Dahoon holly (A)
5. Sweetbay (A)
6. Swamp bay (A)

Subcanopy Trees

1. Swamp dogwood (A)
2. Green haw (N)

Shrubs

1. Myrtle holly (N)

Mesic Hammock

Canopy Trees

1. Most oaks (N or A, depending on species)
2. Elms (A)
3. Hickories (N)
4. American beech (N)
5. Sugar maple (N)
6. American holly (N)
7. Southern magnolia (A)
8. Gumbo limbo (S)
9. Mastic (S)
10. Black ironwood (S)

Subcanopy Trees

1. Flowering dogwood (N)
2. Fringetree (N)
3. Flatwoods plum (N)
4. Sparkleberry (A)
5. Hawthorns (esp. may haw, cockspur, parsley, and littlehip) (N)
6. Blue beech (N)
7. Stoppers (S)
8. Blolly (S)
9. West Indian cherry (S)

Shrubs

1. Carolina holly (N)
2. Yaupon holly (A)
3. Viburnums (N or A, depending on species)
4. Deerberry (N)
5. Dwarf palmetto (N)
6. Needle palm (N)
7. Firebush (S)
8. Tawnyberry holly (S)
9. Marlberry (S)
10. Coffees (S)

Xeric Hammock

Canopy Trees

1. Live oak (A)
2. Sand live oak (A)
3. Southern red cedar (A)
4. Persimmon (A)
5. Sand hickory (N)

Shrubs

1. Saw palmetto (A)
2. Beautyberry (A)
3. Yaupon holly (A)
4. Sparkleberry (N)

Coastal Hammock

Canopy Trees

1. Southern red cedar (A)
2. Live oak (A)
3. Cabbage palm (A)
4. Southern magnolia (N)
5. Gumbo limbo (S)
6. Mastic (S)
7. Black ironwood (S)

Subcanopy Trees

1. Saffron plum (S)
2. Stoppers (S)
3. Blolly (S)

Shrubs

1. Yaupon holly (A)
2. Wax myrtle (A)
3. Florida privet (A)
4. White indigoberry (S)

Tropical Hammock

Trees

1. Cabbage palm (A)
2. Live oak (A)
3. Figs (S)
4. Gumbo limbo (S)
5. Mastic (S)
6. Black ironwood (S)

Subcanopy Trees

1. Stoppers (S)
2. Pigeon plum (S)
3. Willow bustic (S)

Shrubs

1. Tawnyberry holly (S)
2. Spicewood (S)
3. Strongbarks (S)

Design Considerations

I hope this discussion of Florida's native communities provides a useful starting point for planning a landscape and developing a design. Once you have decided how you want the various areas of your landscape to look, you can develop a design around them. With a design, you can choose a plant palette. I firmly believe that this planning and designing process needs to be a personal effort based on your sense of aesthetics and the types of wildlife in which you are most interested. Don't be intimidated by lack of a master plan to start with. Start with the information in this book and embrace the opportunity to create. Never fear the need to tinker with what you've done, to improve on what you've started, or to alter your direction a bit once you see where things are heading. There is no "right" landscape, and, no matter what you plan for, you will ultimately desire to change some of it as time goes by. Frankly, I wouldn't know what to do with myself if I didn't have a little to do each week in my own landscape, something to change or try differently. Dive in with both feet, but only after careful planning and a bit of knowledge. I hope that some of that knowledge has been gained from the pages you have just read. The rest will come from experience. Explore regional parks and natural areas, be observant of what is around you, and seek like-minded folks with whom to share your experiences. A good place to start would be the local chapter of the Florida Native Plant Society. Most importantly, teach others what you have learned, and always remain open to learning more.

Conclusion

For far too many, landscapes are simply spaces to put a house. We dress up the spaces to show off our homes and to advertise that we are good citizens. We pour in huge amounts of energy and money and receive very little in return. The dollars we spend to water and fertilize conventional lawns ultimately end up as yard waste, then we spend even more for someone to cart it all off. Our yards are not a source of joy or a place to explore, but a tiring carousel of never-ending work for no good purpose.

Thankfully, more and more of us are seeking ways to reconnect with the natural world. We have a deep-seated fascination with it and a desire to have it accessible.

I believe we are at a remarkable and exciting tipping point that calls for revolutionary change in our approach to landscaping. As we sit in the comfort of our air-conditioned homes, admiring the world of nature on television and looking out the window to gauge whether we need to turn on the watering system or break out the mower, wildlife in Florida and elsewhere continue to decline at alarming rates.

Though we care about this problem, we have looked to others to fix it. We have not made it personal. It has not been our responsibility—but the problem *is* us and ours to fix. Homeowners in Florida are land managers of some of the most significant swaths of potential wildlife habitat in the nation. Habitat loss resulting from clearing of natural lands is within our scope of influence. It is something we can affect. While some wildlife will never adapt to developed landscapes, far too many species have declined needlessly. Though we have set aside millions of acres of Florida's wild lands for wildlife, it has not been enough to restore the habitat we unnecessarily lost through an unenlightened approach to urban landscaping—and it will never be enough to repair the connectivity we have lost by carving the state into developed and undeveloped fragments.

A female summer tanager stops during spring migration at a central Florida backyard landscaped for wildlife. Photo by Christina Evans, with permission.

We plant our yards. That is not the problem. The problem is that we have not planted them for any ecological purpose.

It is my fervent hope that we will lose this lethargy, seize this moment in time, and accept the responsibility to repair the damage—one yard at a time. We can make our landscapes better wildlife habitat and, by doing so, stave off some of the impacts of urban development. At the same time, we will make the areas where we live and work better habitats for ourselves, too. Instead of loading the family into the car for a trip to a local nature park, we might grab our binoculars and cameras for a safari in our own yard. There is no reason this can't happen and no reason it shouldn't. My friends Christina Evans and Stan Czaplicki have documented more song-birds in their home landscape than the local Audubon Society has in any of our nearby nature parks—and they are just beginning.

At times, we appear conditioned to accept the status quo and power-less to effect change. The tasks ahead are monumental, and it is easy to see why so many want to wish it away with inaction. Despite the ecological challenges, we can make significant differences by taking one small step forward and reconnecting our yards to nature. In doing so, we may dis-cover ourselves as surely as we discover the wildlife that will eventually appear.

Happy gardening and best wishes.

Additional Resources

Books

About Florida Natural History

Alden, P., R. Cech, R. Keen, A. Leventer, G. Nelson, and W. Zomlefer. 1998. *Field Guide to Florida*. National Audubon Society. New York: Alfred Knopf. 447 pp.

Lantz, P. S., and W. A. Hale. 2006. *The Young Naturalist's Guide to Florida*. Sarasota: Pineapple Press. 195 pp.

Myers, R. L., and J. J. Ewel. 1990. *Ecosystems of Florida*. Orlando: University of Central Florida Press. 775 pp.

Perry, J., and J. G. Perry. 1998. *The Nature of Florida*. Athens: University of Georgia Press. 238 pp.

Valentine, J., and D. B. Means. 2006. *Florida Magnificent Wilderness: State Lands, Parks, and Natural Areas*. Sarasota: Pineapple Press. 145 pp.

Whitney, E., D. B. Means, and A. Rudloe. 2004. *Priceless Florida: Natural Systems and Native Species*. Sarasota: Pineapple Press. 423 pp.

About Wildlife Gardening

Buchanan, C. 1999. *The Wildlife Sanctuary Garden*. Berkeley: Ten Speed Press. 209 pp.

Huegel, C. N. 1995. *Florida Plants for Wildlife: A Selection Guide to Native Trees and Shrubs*. Orlando: Florida Native Plant Society. 118 pp.

Leys, M., and R. Leys. 2000. *Living with Wildlife: Create Wildlife Habitat No Matter Where You Live*. Iola, Wis.: Krause Publications. 230 pp.

Marinelli, J. 2008. *The Wildlife Gardener's Guide*. Brooklyn: Brooklyn Botanic Garden All-Region Guides. 119 pp.

Proctor, N. 1986. *Garden Birds: How to Attract Birds to Your Garden*. Emmaus, Pa.: Rodale. 160 pp.

Schaefer, J. M., and G. W. Tanner. 1998. *Landscaping for Florida's Wildlife: Recreating Native Ecosystems in Your Own Backyard*. Gainesville: University Press of Florida. 96 pp.

Schneck, M. 1992. *Your Backyard Wildlife Garden: How to Attract and Identify Wildlife in Your Yard*. Emmaus, Pa.: Rodale. 160 pp.

Seidenberg, C. 1995. *The Wildlife Garden: Planning Backyard Habitats*. Jackson: University Press of Mississippi. 322 pp.

Zickefoose, J. 2001. *The Bird-Friendly Backyard: Natural Gardening for Birds: Simple Ways to Create a Bird Haven*. Emmaus, Pa.: Rodale. 244 pp.

About Wildlife and Native Plants

Martin, A. C., H. S. Zim, and A. L. Nelson. 1951. *American Wildlife & Plants: A Guide to Wildlife Food Habits*. Reprint, New York: Dover, 1961. 500 pp.

Miller, J. H., and K. V. Miller. 2005. *Forest Plants of the Southeast and Their Wildlife Uses*. Athens: University of Georgia Press. 454 pp.

Tallamy, D. W. 2007. *Bringing Nature Home: How Native Plants Sustain Wildlife in Our Gardens*. Portland, Ore.: Timber Press. 288 pp.

About Native Plant Landscaping and Gardening

Diekelmann, J., and R. Schuster. 2002. *Natural Landscaping: Designing with Native Plant Communities*. 2nd ed. Madison: University of Wisconsin Press. 301 pp.

Jameson, M. and R. Moyroud, eds. 1991. *Xeric Landscaping with Florida Native Plants*. San Antonio, Fla.: Association of Florida Native Nurseries. 67 pp.

Stein, S. 1997. *Planting Noah's Garden: Further Adventures in Backyard Ecology*. Boston: Houghton Mifflin. 448 pp.

Walton, D., and L. Schiller. 2007. *Natural Florida Landscaping: Using Native Plants for a Beautiful, Life-Supporting, and Environmentally Sensitive Landscape*. Sarasota: Pineapple Press. 110 pp.

Wasowski, S., and A. Wasowski. 1994. *Gardening with Native Plants of the South*. Dallas: Taylor Publishing. 196 pp.

Organizations

Association of Florida Native Nurseries (AFNN)
P.O. Box 434
Melrose, FL 32666-0434
321-917-1960
http://www.afnn.org

Audubon of Florida
Florida State Office
444 Brickell Avenue, Suite 850
Miami, FL 33131
305-371-6399
http://www.audubonofflorida.org

Florida Native Plant Society
P.O. Box 278
Melbourne, FL 32902-0278
321-271-6702
http://www.fnps.org

Florida Wildlife Federation
P.O. Box 6870
Tallahassee, FL 32314
850-942-4431
http://www.fwfonline.org

National Wildlife Federation
11100 Wildlife Center Dr.
Reston, VA 20190
800-822-9919
http://www.nwf.org

Index

Bold indicates a page with a photograph

Craig Huegel is a wildlife biologist, ecological consultant, and lifelong gardener with a special interest in the relationship between plants and animals. He helped establish the Cooperative Urban Wildlife Program at the University of Florida in 1987 and has been deeply involved in educating the public about Florida's wildlife and native plants ever since.